The Bridgestone
100 Best Places to Stay in Ireland

2011 EDITION

www.bridgestoneguides.com

THE BRIDGESTONE

100 BEST
PLACES TO STAY
IN IRELAND 2011

JOHN MCKENNA - SALLY MCKENNA

ESTRAGON PRESS

FIRST PUBLISHED IN JANUARY 2011

BY ESTRAGON PRESS

DURRUS

COUNTY CORK

© ESTRAGON PRESS

TEXT © JOHN & SALLY MCKENNA

THE MORAL RIGHT OF THE AUTHORS HAS BEEN ASSERTED

ISBN 978-1-906927-05-9

TYPESET IN GILL ALTERNATE AND SABON TO

AN ORIGINAL DESIGN BY NICK CANN

ILLUSTRATIONS BY AOIFE WASSER

PRINTED IN SPAIN BY GRAPHYCEMS

• Front cover photos: top left and bottom right, courtesy Hotel Europe; top right, courtesy The Tannery Townhouse; middle left by Sally McKenna; middle right, courtesy Castlewood House; bottom left, courtesy The Angler's Rest.

• Whilst every effort has been made to ensure that the information given in this book is accurate, the publishers and authors do not accept responsibility for any errors or omissions or for any change in the circumstances of any entries.

WRITTEN & EDITED BY JOHN MCKENNA

CONTRIBUTING EDITORS:

EAMON BARRETT

ORLA BRODERICK

CAROLINE BYRNE

SABRINA CONNEELY

ELIZABETH FIELD

CLAIRE GOODWILLIE

CAROLINE HENNESSY

VALERIE O'CONNOR

JAKKI OWENS

LESLIE WILLIAMS

PUBLISHING EDITOR: SALLY MCKENNA

EDITOR: JUDITH CASEY

EDITORIAL ASSISTANT & WEB PICTURE EDITOR: EVE CLANCY

WEB: fluidedge.ie

FOR:

Jenny Iles

WITH SPECIAL THANKS TO

Des Collins, Colm Conyngham, Pat Curran, Grainne Byrne, Julie Barrett, George Lane, Frank McKevitt, Margaret Deverell, Lelia McKenna, Miguel Sancho, Hugh Stancliffe, Eugene McSweeney, John Ward, Connie McKenna, Sam McKenna, PJ McKenna and all our colleagues at Gill & Macmillan.

Bridgestone is the world's largest tyre and rubber company.

• Founded in Japan in 1931, it currently employs over 100,000 people in Europe, Asia and America and its products are sold in more than 150 countries. Its European plants are situated in France, Spain, Italy, Poland and Turkey.

• Bridgestone manufacture tyres for a wide variety of vehicles from passenger cars and motorcycles, trucks and buses to giant earthmovers and aircraft.

• Many new cars are fitted with Bridgestone tyres during manufacture, including Ford, Toyota, Volkswagen, Mercedes and BMW. Super cars such as Ferrari, Aston Martin and Porsche are also fitted with Bridgestone performance tyres as original equipment.

• Bridgestone commercial vehicle tyres enjoy a worldwide reputation for durability and its aircraft tyres are used by more than 100 airlines.

• In Formula 1 Bridgestone are sole tyre supplier with all the teams now competing on its Potenza racing tyres. Technology developed in the sport has led to increased performance and safety in Bridgestone's road tyres.

x

• Bridgestone tyres are distributed in Ireland by Bridgestone Ireland Ltd, a subsidiary of the multinational Bridgestone Corporation. A wide range of tyres is stocked in its 6,500 square metre central warehouse and its staff provide sales, technical and delivery services all over Ireland.

• Bridgestone tyres are available from First Stop Tyre Centres and tyre dealers throughout Ireland.

For further information:

BRIDGESTONE IRELAND LTD
10 Fingal Bay Business Park
Balbriggan
County Dublin

Tel: + 353 1 841 0000
Fax: + 353 1 841 5245

websites:
www.bridgestone.ie
www.firststop.ie
www.truckpoint.ie

• Coming towards the end of research for this 2011 edition of the best places to stay in Ireland, we checked out a grand, imposing house in the Irish countryside. It was lovely. Majestic, grand, beautifully sited, comfortable, with everything one might need or could need.

• There was, however, just one problem. The owners had no philosophy when it came to hospitality. They had the house and all the bits, but none of the culture that is the vital social glue of making a house work, of making it hospitable. We found the same thing when trying a house in Dublin: all mod cons, but no soul. Staff playing at being hospitable, but unaware of how to conjure and capture the real thing. Facsimile hospitality.

• Hospitality is an art form, a craft, a profession. But, above all, it is a culture, and it is that culture of hospitality, that philosophy that enshrines care and concern for the guest in a true, meaningful and genuine way, that decides which houses make it into this book.

• So when you stay as a guest of the people featured in this book, we know that, along with everything else that will make your stay a pleasure, there will also be a philosophy. Without it, there is simply a building, not a place to stay.

John & Sally McKenna
Durrus, West Cork, November 2010

"The words 'host' and 'guest' originally meant the same thing. They both derive from Indo-European *ghostis,* 'stranger'. What this single term refers to is not so much the individual people, the host and the guest, as the bond that unites them."

Margaret Visser

• The bond that unites host and guest is one of the most profound things in our culture. Indeed, it may be the very thing that lets us call ourselves "civilised", the recognition that we are all strangers until united by the bond of hospitality, of sharing.

• One of the new entrants in this year's edition expressed their philosophy in this way: "We have no hard and fast rules, and try to bend to please the guest in every way possible. If there is something we can do to make this the very best B&B experience for our guests, we will — that is our attitude and we hope to make a difference with it."

• The urge to "make a difference" is the uniting factor that links all the places to stay featured in this book, be they grand country houses, simple B&Bs or smart hotels. It gives us great pride to be able to introduce such people to you, people who are determined to make your experience "the very best".

hot

classic

new

• The Bridgestone 100 Best Places to Stay in Ireland is arranged alphabetically by county, so it begins with County Carlow, which is followed by County Cavan, and so on. Within the counties, the entries are once again listed alphabetically. Entries in Northern Ireland are itemised alphabetically, at the end of the book. All NI prices are quoted in sterling.

• The contents of the Bridgestone 100 Best Guides are exclusively the result of the authors' deliberations. All meals and accommodation were paid for and any offers of discounts or gifts were refused.

• Many of the places featured in this book are only open during the summer, which means that they can be closed for any given length of time between October and March.

• **PRICES:** Average prices are calculated on the basis of one night's stay for bed and breakfast. Prices are subject to change, and therefore can only represent a guideline.

• **LISTINGS:** In every entry in the book we try to list telephone number, and internet details. We also request details of disabled access, the ability to cater for children, pets, plus any other relevant details.

• **GPS CO-ORDINATES:** We have printed co-ordinates as provided to us by the various establishments, written in Decimal Degrees Format. The Bridgestone Guides, however, can accept no responsibility for the ultimate accuracy of the co-ordinates provided to us.

• **TELEPHONE NUMBERS:** Telephone numbers are listed using the international dialling code. If you are calling a number within the country, omit the international code and use the 0.

• **BRIDGESTONE PLAQUES:** Look out for our Bridgestone Plaques, displayed by many of our listed establishments.

KILGRANEY COUNTRY HOUSE

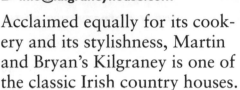

Bryan Leech & Martin Marley
Bagenalstown
County Carlow

📞 **+353 (0) 59-977 5283**
🖱 www.kilgraneyhouse.com
📧 info@kilgraneyhouse.com

Acclaimed equally for its cookery and its stylishness, Martin and Bryan's Kilgraney is one of the classic Irish country houses.

"It is a thoroughly modern country house hotel", wrote the great food writer Annie Bell, back in 1999 when she first visited Bryan and Martin's Kilgraney House. The cooking, said Ms Bell, "sings with wonderfully clear notes". Claire Goodwillie of the Bridgestone parish agrees: her most recent meal at Kilgraney won a single word of praise; "wonderful". Nowhere else is quite like it, nowhere else has such a finely tuned aesthetic in every aspect of the operation, nowhere else has such ageless modernity. One has to applaud the fact that the house itself has changed little over the years, because they got it so right at the start that it hasn't needed to be tampered with. Secondly, Bryan Leech's cooking remains amongst the most intuitive and yet polished country house cooking you can enjoy. When you marry that cooking with the fabulous sense of style that blesses Kilgraney House, then you have a true Irish classic, a thoroughbred country destination.

● **OPEN:** Mar-Nov, Wed-Sun
● **ROOMS:** Six double rooms & two courtyard suites
● **PRICE: B&B** €85-€120 per person sharing. Midweek and aromatherapy packages available.

● **NOTES:** Visa, Mastercard, Amex, Laser. Dinner, 8pm, €52 (Six course), book by noon. Wheelchair access with assistance, please phone to discuss needs. Aroma Spa. Children over 12 only.

● **DIRECTIONS:**
Just off the R705, 6km from Bagenalstown.
GPS 52.653333 -6.957222

STEP HOUSE HOTEL

James & Cait Coady
Main Street, Borris
County Carlow
+353 (0) 59-977 3209
www.stephousehotel.ie
info@stephousehotel.ie

An artful marriage, of hip design and enjoyable but enlivening cooking, has made James and Cait Coady's Step House a County Carlow star.

James and Cait Coady's neat boutique hotel is a great address, marrying a lush, slightly Versace-esque design style with some very good cooking and some very personable service. "Step in the Step House and step out of real life in Borris!" says Claire Goodwillie. And if we do, Claire, then what will we see? "A world of gilt and marble, expansive staircases and muted colours on the walls. A charming reception on arrival boded well, and the bedrooms are spacious, light-filled and airy, with views of Mount Leinster. I could happily have moved in!" The Step House is the sort of place that, after a day's lazy touring, or a day at the horse sales, you can hardly wait to get back to for a drink in the bar, a scrummy dinner – Wexford scallops with lime and asparagus; ham hock and leek terrine; cod brandade with tomato confit; sable Breton with vanilla cream and vanilla ice cream – and then a comfy bed in a commodious, stylish room, and the sleep of the just. Next day, you will want to do it all over again. Perfect.

● **OPEN:** All year
● **ROOMS:** 20 bedrooms
● **PRICE:** B&B from €65-€75 per person sharing. Single supplement €10

● **NOTES:** Visa, Mastercard, Laser. Full wheelchair access. 1808 Bar lunch & dinner, 12.20pm-2pm, 6pm-9.30pm. Cellar Restaurant opens Fri & Sat, 7-10pm

● **DIRECTIONS:**
Borris is in between Carlow and Kilkenny, and the hotel is on the main street in the village.
GPS 52.601244 -6.927553

MacNEAN TOWNHOUSE

Neven & Amelda Maguire
Blacklion
County Cavan
☎ **+353 (0) 71-985 3022**
🖱 **www.macneanrestaurant.com**
✉ **info@macneanrestaurant.com**

Neven and Amelda Maguire are superstars these days, but their feet are rooted in little Blacklion, in County Cavan.

Here is the good news: the MacNean is extending. Having acquired the adjoining building, Neven and Amelda Maguire will be adding a flight of extra rooms to their acclaimed townhouse. This is good news for a simple reason: the MacNean Townhouse tends to be booked for up to 6-8 months in advance – we had to stay in a house down the road on our last trip! – so it's actually the most difficult place to get a booking in Ireland. And if you make the pilgrimage to come to Blacklion to eat in the MacNean Restaurant, then you really do want to stay right here. What will you find when you arrive? A modest, unassuming house in a modest, unassuming village, and pretty, comfortable rooms. And a restaurant and townhouse powered by the most dedicated, enthusiastic staff, who serve some of the best cooking in Europe. Don't make the mistake of staying for one night: to see what this team achieve you need to stay for at least two nights, time to absorb the drama, the theatre, the intensity!

- **OPEN:** All year, except January
- **ROOMS:** Ten rooms
- **PRICE:** B&B €70 per person sharing

- **NOTES:** Visa, Mastercard, Laser. MacNean Restaurant open 6pm-9.30pm Wed-Sat; 1pm & 3.30pm, 7pm-8.30pm Sun (closed Wed low season). Sun Lunch €39, Dinner €70-€85. Vegetarian menu €50

- **DIRECTIONS:**
On the main street in Blacklion.
GPS 54.291361 -7.877739

THE OLDE POST INN

Tara McCann & Gearoid Lynch
Cloverhill, Butler's Bridge
County Cavan
📞 **+353 (0) 47-55555**
🖲 www.theoldepostinn.com
✉ gearoidlynch@eircom.net

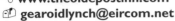

One of the jewels of the borderlands, Tara and Gearoid's Olde Post Inn is a splendid, special place to stay, graced by great cooking and great service.

Tara McCann is one of the best hostesses, and Gearoid Lynch is, for our money, one of the best cooks at work in Ireland today. Together, Ms McCann and Mr Lynch have made their restaurant with rooms, the Olde Post, a sweet, intimate red brick building near Butler's Bridge, into a classy destination, a little jewel in the borderlands. They have worked steadily and consistently to improve and upgrade every aspect of their house, from the conservatory to the guest rooms, but they have never lost their focus on the quality of service and the quality of the cooking whilst they have busied themselves getting their place shipshape. They are helped in their task by some of the very best staff in the business, witty, smart, wholesome people, the kind of staff who have become all too scarce in many Irish destinations. But here they are, working hard, ferrying out Mr Lynch's cooking, and truly lovely, singular, tactile cooking it is, from dinner through to breakfasts, looking after you, making sure you are happy.

- ● **OPEN:** all year, except Christmas
- ● **ROOMS:** Six double rooms.
- ● **PRICE:** B&B €110 per double room

- ● **NOTES:** Olde Post Inn restaurant open 6pm-9pm Tue-Thu, 6pm-9.30pm Fri-Sat, 12.30pm-2.30pm, 5.30pm-8.30pm Sun. Dinner €56, Sun Lunch €35. No wheelchair access.

- ● **DIRECTIONS:**
From Cavan follow N3. At Butler's Bridge, take the N54 and the Olde Post is 3km further, on the right.
GPS 54.0801 -7.3701

CULLINAN'S

James & Carol Cullinan
Doolin
County Clare
📞 + 353 (0) 65-707 4183
🖱 www.cullinansdoolin.com
📧 cullinans@eircom.net

Highly professional and highly personal, James & Carol's restaurant with rooms seems to breathe the very spirit of nimble, artful, busy, darling Doolin.

James and Carol Cullinan's excellent restaurant with rooms in the centre of Doolin is a peachy, professional destination. What is particularly nice about the newer rooms at Cullinan's is their proximity to the river, views of which can be enjoyed from their balconies, and whilst the rooms are compact, floor to ceiling glass walls makes them seem huge. They are chic and stylish, smashing getaways, and both the bedrooms and the public rooms enjoy meticulous housekeeping.

James Cullinan's cooking is based on classic principles and techniques, and good sourcing, good, fresh breads and clean, big flavours make for great eating: john dory with basil-scented whipped potatoes and pancetta and leek carbonara with tomato concentrate; Dijon-crusted monkfish studded with Burren smoked salmon with celeriac mousseline and rocket compote are just two dishes that show the inventiveness and engagement of the kitchen, and those qualities are evident in a super breakfast menu that runs the gamut of good things.

● **OPEN:** mid Feb-mid Dec
● **ROOMS:** Ten double & twin rooms
● **PRICE:** B&B €32.50-€50 per person sharing, €40-€70 single

● **NOTES:**
Visa, Mastercard, Laser. No wheelchair access.
Restaurant open 6pm-9pm (closed Wed & Sun), dinner €30-€45

● **DIRECTIONS:**
At the cross roads, coming down from the school, in centre of Doolin. GPS 53.016111 -9.377222

GREGAN'S CASTLE

Simon Haden & Frederieke McMurray
Ballyvaughan
County Clare
📱 **+ 353 (0) 65 707 7005**
🖱 **www.gregans.ie**
📧 **stay@gregans.ie**

The following is Eamon Barrett's review of Gregan's Castle. A review? Actually, it's not criticism: this is quite simply a love letter.

What is true luxury and how can it be measured? By the length of the swimming pool? By the size of the plasma screen in your room? True luxury is none of these things, it is more akin to true love - that subliminal sense of calm and pure relaxation that come from being truly cared for. Whatever it is - it can be found at Gregan's Castle where a wonderful building in a bucolic setting is matched utterly by a team who truly embrace their task of caring for, and about, the well-being of their guests. Add in a food offering that can hardly be matched in the country and you have arrived at that elusive combination that creates a near-perfect hospitality experience. Afternoon tea would knock the socks off the most expensive Knightsbridge competitor; dinner is breathtaking and doesn't confuse cutting-edge presentation with cutting-edge cooking; the rooms are extremely comfortable and every element of Gregan's Castle is just perfection.

● **OPEN:** 11 Feb-27 November
● **ROOMS:** 20 rooms and suites
● **PRICE:** €160-€320 per room

● **NOTES:** Restaurant open 6pm-9pm Mon-Sat, €65.
Bar lunch available Mon-Sat, from €15.
Bar Lunch & Dinner, €25-€35, Sun.
Burren tours arranged. Wheelchair access.
Croquet pitch.

● **DIRECTIONS:**
3.5 miles outside Ballyvaughan village.
GPS 53.076944 -9.186222

27

WITH GREAT SPAS

1

HOTEL EUROPE
COUNTY KERRY

2

KELLYS RESORT HOTEL
COUNTY WEXFORD

3

KILGRANEY COUNTRY HOUSE
COUNTY CARLOW

4

THE KILLARNEY PARK HOTEL
COUNTY KERRY

5

KNOCKRANNY HOUSE HOTEL
COUNTY MAYO

6

MONART
COUNTY WEXFORD

7

THE MUSTARD SEED
COUNTY LIMERICK

8

NUMBER ONE PERY SQUARE
COUNTY LIMERICK

9

THE PARK HOTEL
COUNTY KERRY

10

TEMPLE
COUNTY WESTMEATH

MORRISSEY'S

Hugh Morrissey
Doonbeg
County Clare

☎ +353 (0) 65-905 5304
🖰 www.morrisseysdoonbeg.com
✉ info@morrisseysdoonbeg.com

Terrific value for money, for both the excellent cooking and the splendid rooms, makes Hugh Morrissey's riverside D'n'D your Co Clare address.

Hugh Morrissey has transformed this lovely pub from a traditional Irish bar into a svelte restaurant with rooms, yet he has somehow managed to keep the graceful ambience of the old place, where four generations of the Morrissey family have plied their trade. The cooking is modern, flavour-filled and very accessible, so it's a great family destination, and when the kids have eaten and escaped off to the riverside to play, you get a chance to drink in the charms of this singular address, and relax. That relaxed air is worth dwelling on, for it's really the signature of Morrissey's, a youthful, laid-back sang-froid that is hard to resist. We have remarked before on the incredible feat that Hugh Morrissey has performed in his stylish d'n'd: from a simple family-run pub that was open for only a few months of the year, he has created a dynamic dinner 'n' duvet – still with a bar, mind you – that now opens fully for ten months of the year. So, lots of chances to pay a visit to south Clare, and drink in its delights.

● **OPEN:** March-Dec
● **ROOMS:** Seven rooms
● **PRICE:** B&B €90 per room, €60 single

● **NOTES:** Visa, Mastercard, Laser, Amex. Pub restaurant opens for lunch, 12.30pm-2.30pm, and dinner, 6pm-9.30pm, €35.

● **DIRECTIONS:**
From Ennis, follow the Kilrush road. In Kilrush follow signs for Kilkee, and then look for the Doonbeg sign. The pub is right beside the bridge in the centre of the village. GPS 52.730861 -9.524353

MOY HOUSE

Antoin O'Looney (owner)
Brid O'Meara (General Manager)
Lahinch, County Clare
📞 +353 (0) 65-708 2800
🖱 www.moyhouse.com
✉ bomeara@moyhouse.com

Brid O'Meara is one of the most dynamic personalities in Irish hospitality, and the pretty Moy House benefits from her drive and determination.

Moy House is the business. Handsome, distinctive, singular, it's a house that unwinds its charms slowly, a quiet, unshowy destination that soon captivates you. Here is Eamon Barrett on a visit to Brid O'Meara's house: "Initially I wasn't sure I liked it. But the more time I spent there, reading, looking out to the rough sea, helping myself to Power's 12-year-old whiskey from the honesty bar, the more I liked it. We had a beautiful room with a built-in window seat and a fabulous bathroom. Lorge chocolates from West Cork were left in the room for us. In the evening, there were slippers and candles lighting. We had our own turf fire in the room, for goodness sake! At breakfast the next morning there was a taste of the level that Moy is pitched at with truly superb service and an excellent breakfast of scrambled egg with mushroom accompanied by really good brown bread. Staff were excellent - again that all-important welcome from Brid - and nothing we asked for was too much trouble."

● **OPEN:** Feb-Dec
● **ROOMS:** Nine rooms
● **PRICE:** B&B €185-€280 per double room, Suite €270-€360, Single €145-€175

● **NOTES:**
Visa, Mastercard, Laser. Special offers Nov-May. Special packages/group rates available. Resident's dinner, €55.

● **DIRECTIONS:**
Moy House is located about 1.5km south of Lahinch town, on the Miltown Malbay road. Shannon Airport is 1 hour's drive. GPS 52.951381 -9.346285

SHEEDY'S

John & Martina Sheedy
Lisdoonvarna
County Clare

☎ +353 (0) 65-707 4026
🖳 www.sheedys.com
📧 info@sheedys.com

Sheedy's is one of the bestest, nicest family-run hotels in Ireland. Happily for us all, it's as fine today in the present as it has been for generations.

Sheedy's is one of those discreet, intimate, family-run hotels that once characterised the hospitality culture of Ireland, but which have become all too rare in recent decades. Happily, that meticulous, subtle and charming culture of Irish hospitality lives on in this family hotel, thanks to Martina Sheedy's polite, shy service, and John Sheedy's utterly lovely, utterly logical cooking. Everything is done by hand, and such care gladdens the heart on every visit. Sheedy's does things the old-fashioned way. "All dishes are cooked fresh to order" it says at the foot of their dinner menu, which also describes their dedicated local suppliers, and that cooked to order care even extends to breakfast, every part of which is cooked individually and served by the team. John and Martina Sheedy have to work hard to do this intensive hands-on hospitality, and it is the happy guest who benefits in this pretty and simple hotel. Simple it may be, but its heart is the very heart of hospitality, the essence of Irish generosity, and simple deliciousness.

● **OPEN:** from Easter to early October
● **ROOMS:** Eight rooms and three junior suites
● **PRICE:** €99-€170 per room

● **NOTES:** All major cards accepted.
One room wheelchair accessible.
Restaurant open during summer, and ring off season.
Special offers available all year, telephone for details.

● **DIRECTIONS:**
200m from the centre of Lisdoonvarna, on the road going out towards the wells.
GPS 53.02771 -9.28909

VAUGHAN LODGE

Michael & Maria Vaughan
Lahinch
County Clare
📞 +353 (0) 65-708 1111
🖰 www.vaughanlodge.ie
✉ info@vaughanlodge.ie

The Vaughan dynasty has practised the art of hospitality in Lahinch for generations now, and Michael and Maria continue the noble tradition.

There isn't a more professionally-focused and orientated couple in the hospitality business than Michael and Maria Vaughan, and their latest upgrade of the restaurant menu in the Lodge, with chef James Coffey wielding the pans in the kitchen, is another sign that when the going gets tough, the smart ones just up their game and get to a higher place. The cooking is modern and hip: roast prawns with slow-cooked pork belly; seared scallops with Sauternes sauce; halibut with lobster velouté; pistachio and polenta cake. This hospitality is vital. You don't build hotels and places to stay out of bricks and mortar: hospitality is what builds hotels, the rest is big boxes with bedrooms: bed factories as they are known in the trade. What you get in Vaughan Lodge, however, thanks to Michael and Maria is a narrative of hospitality that extends back through four generations of their family, working in this town. And that narrative of hospitality, that history, that culture, is why Vaughan Lodge works. It's the tradition!

● **OPEN:** Apr-Nov
● **ROOMS:** 20 rooms, all en suite
● **PRICE:** €85-€135 per person sharing.
Single €130-€220

● **NOTES:** All major cards accepted. Full wheelchair access. Restaurant, dinner €47. Open 6.30pm-9.15pm Tue-Sat. Private car parking. Loc8 code K20-7303MF

● **DIRECTIONS:**
From Ennis, take the N85 to Ennistymon, turn left onto N67 to Lahinch, and the hotel is just inside the 50km zone on the left. GPS 52.933889 -9.341111

AHERNE'S

The Fitzgibbon family
163 North Main Street
Youghal, East Cork
📱 **+353 (0) 24-92424**
🖰 **www.ahernes.com**
📠 **ahernes@eircom.net**

The Fitzgibbon family understand the art of looking after you better than almost anyone else: just turn up and surrender to their relaxed charm.

In Aherne's they look after you with an easy charm that masks a rigorous professionalism, and prepare sumptuous breakfasts which are amongst the finest you will enjoy anywhere. They serve great food, both in the bar and in the restaurant, where David Fitzgibbon's cooking has long been one of the glories of east Cork. Aherne's, then, is the archetype of the coaching inn for the 21st century, a place of little ceremony, but much accomplishment, a place where they have honed their art for generations, but where the practice of that art always feels fresh and motivated. Sprezzatura, is the term the Italians would use for it: effortless achievement. Like many coaching inns, the location isn't special, and Aherne's is hard by the side of the road at the east end of Youghal. But you need only walk in the door to feel quite removed from the town, and this cocooning atmosphere is one of the secrets of Aherne's success. The rooms congratulate this special atmosphere with design that is classic, and timeless.

● **OPEN:** All year, except Christmas
● **ROOMS:** 12 rooms, all en suite
● **PRICE:** €65-€95 per person sharing, Single from €110

● **NOTES:**
All major cards accepted. Lunch/Dinner in restaurant or bar. Wheelchair access. Secure parking. Check web for offers.

● **DIRECTIONS:**
Aherne's is well signposted in Youghal, a large yellow building on the right-hand side if travelling eastwards. GPS 52.957122 -7.852028

ASHLEE LODGE

Anne & John O'Leary
Tower, Blarney
County Cork
📞 **+353 (0) 21-438 5346**
🖰 **www.ashleelodge.com**
📧 **info@ashleelodge.com**

Anne and John's Ashlee Lodge is your home from home when visiting Blarney. On second thoughts, if only home was as comfortable as lovely Ashlee.

Anne and John O'Leary describe Ashlee as a four-star private hotel, but one of the secrets of their house is the fact that it doesn't feel anything like a conventional hotel, and it doesn't look like an hotel, though it does enjoy hotel levels of decor and comfort.

But what no other comparable four-star hotel could offer is the incomparable service that this dedicated couple practice. Nothing is too much of a problem for these splendid people, and the O'Learys even seem, at times, to be mind-readers, capable of knowing what it is you need, or might need, or might like, even before you articulate the request yourself.

Their care extends to every detail of Ashlee – the superb cooking they offer, enjoyed in the warming, bright conservatory; the level of comfort in public and private rooms; the cosy drawing room with its honour bar. Above all, there is the constant presence of Anne and John themselves, as they prove themselves masters of the art of hospitality in each and every detail of Ashlee.

● **OPEN:** 20 Jan-20 Dec
● **ROOMS:** 10 rooms, all en suite, made up of six executive rooms, two mini suites and two master suites
● **PRICE:** €89 for standard room, €120 for mini suite, €180 for master suite, per person sharing

● **NOTES:** All major cards accepted. Dinner Tue-Sat, €45. Wheelchair access. No facilities for children. Secure parking. Pet friendly. Outdoor hot tub.

● **DIRECTIONS:**
From Blarney, take the R617 for 1.5km to Tower.
GPS 51.924328 -8.612233

BALLYMALOE HOUSE

The Allen family
Shanagarry, Midleton
East Cork
☎ **+353 (0) 21-465 2531**
🖰 **www.ballymaloe.com**
✉ **res@ballymaloe.ie**

The Allen family's Ballymaloe House represents an ideal Ireland: modest, charming, pastoral, lovely.

With the Grain Store hosting excellent concerts of all styles, and new farm cottages and apartments created out in the yard – last time here we stayed as a family in the lovely Tower house, and it was just great – Ballymaloe is slowly, organically extending beyond the original family home where guests traditionally stay. But whether you want to do some self-catering, or enjoy all the aspects of the house, the fact remains that Ballymaloe's star remains undimmed. The Allen family quietly and modestly go about their business, which is, frankly, to be the best in the business. New family members arrive and contribute their skills and gifts to this mighty enterprise. The cooking is as fine as ever, the service understated. Ballymaloe is a bit like what they say about *The Irish Times*, when you think of it: others exist to make money, but Ballymaloe makes money in order to exist. It's a profound difference, and it goes a long way to explaining the unique, ageless charm and character of Ireland's most famous address.

● **OPEN:** All year
● **ROOMS:** 30 rooms. No suites
● **PRICE:** B&B €60-€110 per person sharing. Single €110-€130

● **NOTES:** All major cards accepted. Dinner 7pm-9.30pm, €70 (buffet dinner on Sun night, 7.30pm). Recommended for vegetarians. Children welcome, early dinner. Parking. Two wheelchair-friendly bedrooms.

● **DIRECTIONS:**
From Cork take N25 to exit for Whitegate R630, follow signs for R629. GPS 51.868297 -8.0837

BALLYVOLANE HOUSE

Justin & Jenny Green
Castlelyons, Fermoy
North Cork

☏ **+353 (0) 25-36349**
🖰 **www.ballyvolanehouse.ie**
✉ **info@ballyvolanehouse.ie**

Justin and Jenny's Ballyvolane House has, above all its many charms, the most perfect country ambience.

Goodness me, but Justin and Jenny Green are moving quickly in Ballyvolane. In addition to opening the hugely successful O'Brien Chop House in Lismore as a stand-alone restaurant, they have newly opened a café called The Canteen at the Livinghealth clinic in Mitchelstown. How do they do it? Quite simply, they understand exactly how to give a destination – a country house, a café, a restaurant – just exactly the feeling and ambience that you want. This means that Ballyvolane feels exactly the way you want a country house to feel: timeless, pristine, cultured, sheerly beautiful, welcoming, hospitable, friendly, out of time. "For my money, one of THE stellar country houses, and in the ascendant." Our editor Eamon Barrett's summation of Ballyvolane was ecstatic, but it is no more than every guest who stays at this most beautiful house finds themselves saying when it is time to leave. Ballyvolane is quite simply superb, and offers one of the greatest country house experiences you can enjoy anywhere.

● **OPEN:** 1 Jan-23 Dec
● **ROOMS:** Six rooms, all en suite
● **PRICE:** B&B €75-€105 per person sharing. Single €120-€125

● **NOTES:** Visa, Mastercard, Laser, Amex. Dinner 8pm, €50, communal table. Private car park. Children welcome. Self catering also available. Pet friendly.

● **DIRECTIONS:**
From the N8, south just after Rathcormac, take the turn to Midleton and look for the sign for the house.
GPS 51.096822 -7.530917

BLINDGATE HOUSE

Maeve Coakley
Blindgate, Kinsale
West Cork
📱 **+353 (0) 21-477 7858**
🖥 **www.blindgatehouse.com**
📧 **info@blindgatehouse.com**

Maeve Coakley's pretty house is a great address in Kinsale, with a perfect location in the quiet end of town, lovely cooking, and fabulous style.

We have always loved the style of Maeve Coakley's house, and the fact that its somewhat conventional exterior hides one of the most superbly designed interiors of any house in this entire book.

But style doesn't win out over comfort in Blindgate, and so this is a very cosy house to hang out in, and not one of those design traps that involves you suffering for someone else's art. As such, Blindgate is a terrific base for staying, relaxing and exploring, enjoying all the best of Kinsale whilst just being far enough up the hill to ensure peace and quiet when the town is at full tilt, but also allowing you to head out both eastwards and westwards through County Cork to sample the incredible varieties of the county, both geographically and gastronomically. Breakfasts are just as stylish and fine as the design, setting you up for the perfect day. The designer John Rocha operates by the maxim that "If you get the design right at the start, you don't need to change it later". Blindgate shows how to do just that.

● **OPEN:** Mar-Dec
● **ROOMS:** 11 rooms (seven twin rooms, three standard double rooms & one superior double)
● **PRICE:** B&B €100-€160 per room

● **NOTES:** Visa, Mastercard, Amex. No dinner. Wheelchair access with assistance, but no walk-in showers. Enclosed parking.

● **DIRECTIONS:**
200m past St Multose Church – just up the hill from the Kinsale Gourmet Store.
GPS 51.703842 -8.5253852

FORTVIEW HOUSE

Violet Connell
Gurtyowen, Toormore
Goleen, West Cork
📱 **+353 (0) 28-35324**
🖥 **www.fortviewhousegoleen.com**
📧 **fortviewhousegoleen@eircom.net**

"Probably the best B&B we have ever stayed in", says Eamon Barrett of Bridgestone Central.

"Here it is, in a single property, the archetype Irish B&B in all its wonder", writes Eamon Barrett, enjoying Fortview on his 2010 staycation. "The MOST friendly welcome, the MOST impressive breakfast you will ever come across. A warren of comfortable rooms, and the most wonderful care. Probably the best B and B we have ever stayed in." Wow! And there's more: "Violet Connell is one of the nicest people you will ever meet and we loved every minute staying in this smashing house. The great crime of the government's failure to act on the rates being offered by NAMA, Zombie, call them what you like hotels, is that those involved in true hospitality, those who have that gift of being able to be truly themselves and invite and appreciate guests staying in their homes, will be lost, as unsustainable room rates in failed hotels supported by failed banks will simply drive them out of business." Let's hope it doesn't happen, Eamon, because we need all the Violets and Fortviews we can get!

- **OPEN:** 1 Apr-1 Oct
- **ROOMS:** Three rooms, all en suite
- **PRICE:** B&B €50 per person sharing

- **NOTES:** No credit cards accepted. Dinner strictly by prior arrangement only, €35. Two self-catering houses available. No wheelchair access. Enclosed car park. Children over 6yrs welcome in house (all ages self-catering).

- **DIRECTIONS:**
Signposted 2km from Toormore on the main Durrus road (R591). 12km from Durrus, 9km from Goleen. GPS 51.539889 -9.640589

GARNISH HOUSE

Con & Hansi Lucey
Western Road, Cork City
County Cork
☎ **+353 (0) 21-427 5111**
🖰 **www.garnish.ie**
✉ **info@garnish.ie**

"It is the best place in the world", an American friend confided to us, regarding Hansi Lucey's Cork city B&B. Garnish House is worth the praise.

Hansi Lucey's house brings out the effusive in guests who arrive here. "The tea, scones and chocolate cakes when you first arrive – bliss!", a correspondent wrote to us recently, just one in a long line of letters and mails of praise stretching back through the years. Well, how could anyone resist that? Others might give you scones. Or cake. But Hansi gives you both. Garnish is always about the extra choice: would you like some fish for breakfast? Eggs Benedict? An Irish breakfast with three rashers, two sausages, roulade of black pudding, potato cake, hash brown, fried egg, fried tomato, and some mushrooms? What about an omelette with some potato wedges? Or a vegetarian rissole? (There are always great vegetarian choices in Garnish). And what about a fruit-filled pancake to finish? The Garnish House breakfast is a cornucopia of good things, a trove of stunning generosity. Is it, indeed, the best place in the world? Well, why not check it out, and then drop us a line with your opinion.

● **OPEN:** All year
● **ROOMS:** 30 rooms, including four apartments
● **PRICE:** B&B €38-€52 per person sharing, €59-€80 single, €129 family room

● **NOTES:** All major cards accepted. No dinner. Limited wheelchair access. Enclosed car parking. Children welcome. Self-catering accommodation available.

● **DIRECTIONS:**
Five minutes' walk from the city centre, opposite UCC. GPS 51.8957 -8.4886

THE GLEN

Diana & Guy Scott
Kilbrittain
West Cork
☎ +353 (0) 23-49862
🖱 www.glencountryhouse.ie
📧 info@glencountryhouse.com

The Glen is a beautiful mid-nineteenth century country house in the most gorgeous West Cork location. And that's just the start of what makes it special.

What makes The Glen, Diana and Guy Scott's manor house close to the coast at Kilbrittain, so special? It's not simply the beauty of the house, although it is very beautiful, or its impressive vintage: it dates from 1860, and is appropriately creeper-clad. It's not even Diana's capacious skills as hostess, at which she is a whizz. No, there is something else going on here, in this beautiful house which unfolds itself at the end of a long avenue of mature trees, just a stone's throw from the sea. The Glen is one of those places that seem to tap into our need and desire for nostalgia, so there is something fundamentally primal about it. You might have been reared in a two-up, two-down in Stoneybatter, but when you step in the door of The Glen you will feel you not only belong here, you will feel you were somehow born here. It's the nostalgia we feel for an imagined, privileged childhood, no matter how contrary the reality may be. And that is why The Glen is so special: your inner child is released in this special place to stay.

● **OPEN:** April-Nov
● **ROOMS:** Four rooms and one family unit
● **PRICE:** B&B €60 per person sharing, one night, €55 two nights, €45 three nights.

● **NOTES:** Visa, Mastercard, Laser. No dinner. No wheelchair access. Secure car parking. Family unit is for two adults and two children under 16yrs. Pet friendly.

● **DIRECTIONS:**
Signposted from the R6099 approximately half way between Clonakilty and Kinsale.
GPS 51.533933 -8.700794

FOR ROMANCE

1

BROOK'S HOTEL
COUNTY DUBLIN

2

GREGAN'S CASTLE
COUNTY CLARE

3

THE HERON'S REST
COUNTY GALWAY

4

INIS MEÁIN SUITES
COUNTY GALWAY

5

KILCOLMAN RECTORY
COUNTY CORK

6

THE MILL
COUNTY DONEGAL

7

MOORFIELD LODGE
COUNTY DONEGAL

8

NEWTOWN HOUSE
COUNTY CORK

9

THE OLD CONVENT
COUNTY TIPPERARY

10

THE ROSS
COUNTY KERRY

GORT NA NAIN FARM VEGETARIAN GUESTHOUSE

Lucy Stewart & Ultan Walsh
Ballyherkin. Nohoval, County Cork
📱 **+353 (0) 21-477 0647**
🖥 www.gortnanain.com
📧 lucy@gortnanain.com

There is only one question about Gort na Nain, says Caroline Hennessy: When are we going back?

Something new

Staying at Gort na Nain with Lucy and Ultan is like staying with some of your most hospitable friends: there's a warm welcome when you arrive at their delightful, eco-friendly farmhouse, you always get a comfortable room, ready-equipped with great music, books and herbal teas, and, to top it all off, they are both amazing cooks. Only the best of ingredients are used, for on this nine-acre smallholding the couple grow high-quality vegetables for top Cork restaurants. Depending on what's good in the garden, a meal might start with beetroot, Ardsallagh goats' cheese and pecan ravioli, followed by roast pumpkin and borlotti bean molé with crushed potatoes and creamed cavolo nero. Dessert? A baked blackberry cheesecake, with just-picked berries from nearby brambles. Don't let the informal setting fool you: this is first-class cooking, well presented, beautifully plated, and – just incidentally – vegetarian. Meals are served family-style with the hosts and other guests, and Gort na Nain is simply superb.

● **OPEN:** All year
● **ROOMS:** Three rooms, all en suite
● **PRICE:** €85-€95 for two people sharing, €60 single

● **NOTES:** Vegetarian dinner, for guests only, three courses €30. Bring your own wine. Picnic baskets.
Pet friendly (booking essential)
Loc8 Code WBJ-13-SY9

● **DIRECTIONS:**
Take the airport road out of Cork. Turn left at Belgooly. Gort na Nain is five minutes further on up this road.

GOUGANE BARRA HOTEL

Neil & Katy Lucey
Gougane Barra, Macroom
County Cork
☎ **+353 (0) 26-47069**
🖱 **www.gouganebarrahotel.com**
✉ **gouganebarrahotel@eircom.net**

The GBH is the gentlest, most elemental of Irish hotels, set in a most beautiful part of beautiful West Cork.

Neil and Katy's GB Hotel is one of the nicest hotels in Ireland. If you thought that the sort of hotel where she cooks in the kitchen, and where he meets and greets the guests, had vanished under the tsunami of zombie hotels that now litter the country, then a trip to the lake of Gougane Barra will restore your soul, your sanity, and your faith in true Irish hospitality.

Mrs Lucey's food is pure lovely; a timeless, fashion-free style of cooking that fills your heart with joy as it fills your belly with goodness. Mr Lucey is an hotelier of the old school – polite, charming, modest, attentive to every need. We love the simplicity of the rooms, we love walking in the woods, and by the beautiful, peaceful lake, and we love especially the Theatre by the Lake in summertime, when a evening of d 'n' d 'n' d – dinner and drama and duvet – is one of the best experiences you can enjoy in Ireland. Priceless, just priceless, the pure expression of Irish hospitality at its simple, quiet best.

● **OPEN:** early Apr-late Oct
● **ROOMS:** 26 rooms
● **PRICE:** €99 B&B per room

● **NOTES:** All major cards accepted. Theatre by the Lake opens mid July-late Aug. No wheelchair access. Restaurant opens breakfast & dinner from 6pm. Special rate for two nights plus one dinner.

● **DIRECTIONS:**
Take the R584 between Macroom & Bantry, then the L4643, following signs for Gougane Barra after the Pass. GPS 51.833333 -9.316667

GROVE HOUSE

Katarina Runske
Colla Road, Schull
West Cork
📞 +353 (0) 28-28067
🖰 www.grovehouseschull.com
📧 info@grovehouseschull.com

With young Nico firing out homely and delicious food in the Grove House kitchens, a third generation of the Runske family steps into the limelight.

Katarina Runske is a human dynamo, one of those extraordinary people whose elemental energy is astounding to an outsider. How she does all she does in this lovely destination that is Grove House, we simply do not know, but she runs the house, the restaurant, the gallery and all else as if it is just an average day's work. Which, to Ms Runske, is just what it is. With her smart young son, Nico, handling things in the kitchen, Ms Runske has moved the lovely Grove House centre stage in the hospitality culture of Schull, and Nico is cut from the same cloth as his Mum: he makes it all seem easy, and he learns at lightning speed. It's a cliché to say that Grove somehow summarises the classy bohemianism of Schull but, to tell the truth, Grove somehow summarises the classy bohemianism of Schull. It's slightly patrician, slightly eccentric, 100% West Cork. And keep an eye on young Nico as he gets more confidence rattling the pots and pans: this is a serious cooking talent who will make a big splash.

- **OPEN:** all year
- **ROOMS:** Five double rooms
- **PRICE:** B&B €40-€60 per person sharing. Single supplement €25

- **NOTES:** Visa, Laser, Mastercard, Amex. Restaurant open daily in summer, weekends only off season. Dinner always available for guests, from €22.50. Private parking. No wheelchair access.

- **DIRECTIONS:**
Take left opposite AIB, turn onto Colla Road, Grove House is about 500 metres on the right-hand side.

KILCOLMAN RECTORY

Sarah Gornall
Enniskeane
County Cork
📱 **+353 (0) 23-882 2913**
🖰 **www.kilcolmanrectory.com**
📁 **sarahjgornall@eircom.net**

Sarah Gornall is chef, gardener and designer and achieves all with a sprezzatura nonchalance in one of West Cork's most beautiful places to stay.

Sarah Gornall has trained as a chef, as a gardener, and as an interior designer, and it's as if all of her education in these disciplines has been designed to lead her to create this impeccably beautiful house, one of the smartest arrivals on the Irish hospitality scene in recent years. She is one of those rare people who really can create feng shui by putting the right object in the right place in order to create the right aesthetic: Kilcolman has jumped straight from *The World of Interiors*. "Sarah Gornall is someone who not only espouses perfection, but somehow makes perfection look easy." That's how the *Irish Examiner*'s Mary Leland summed up Sarah Gornall's modus operandi in this achingly beautiful 19th-century rectory. There is a word – a superb Italian word coined by Baldassare Castiglione in his *The Book of the Courtier* in 1528 – for what Ms Gornall achieves and the way in which she achieves it: sprezzatura: the nonchalance that conceals effort. The effort behind Kilcolman is huge. You'd never guess.

● **OPEN:** all year
● **ROOMS:** One double/twin en suite, and three double/twins sharing two adjacent shower rooms.
● **PRICE:** B&B €75 per person, sharing. Single €80

● **NOTES:** No credit cards. Dinner €45, advance booking essential.

● **DIRECTIONS:** From Bandon take the Clonakilty road. Turn right after Hosfords Garden Centre. Follow road straight through a crossroads. Carry on until you come to Y junction. Take left fork, and the entrance is third on the right. GPS 51.73128 -8.86649

KNOCKEVEN HOUSE

John & Pam Mulhaire
Rushbrooke, Cobh
County Cork
📱 **+353 (0) 21-481 1778**
🖱 **www.knockevenhouse.com**
📧 **info@knockevenhouse.com**

John and Pam are masters
of the great tradition of
Irish hospitality, and epito-
mise it in Knockeven.

"The finest traditions of country house hospitality."
That's what John and Pam Mulhaire promise that you
will experience and enjoy in their gorgeous 1840
manor house, just outside Cobh. The interesting thing
about their evocation of the tradition of hospitality,
however, is the fact that Pam and John are, relatively
speaking, ingenues at the game, having only opened
their house up in 2005. But, however they acquired
their mastery of the tradition, masters of it the Mul-
haires most certainly are. This is a superb destination,
distinguished by superb housekeeping, characterised by
the voluble vivacity of Pam's personality, and galvanised
by her stunningly delicious breakfasts – the scrambled
eggs that Pam prepares are amongst the very best
in Ireland, and her buffet table is a feast for the eyes,
the senses and the appetite. Wrap all these elements
together in this special house, and you have a place you
want to wrap yourself in, savouring every moment of
the tradition of great Irish hospitality.

● **OPEN:** all year, except Christmas
● **ROOMS:** Four double rooms
● **PRICE:** B&B €50-€60 per person sharing. Single
€60-€75

● **NOTES:** Visa, Mastercard, Laser accepted.
No wheelchair access. Loc8 W8P -49-MD8

● **DIRECTIONS:**
Leave the N25, turn onto the R624, direction Cobh. Pass
Fota, cross over bridge, take first right. At Great Gas
Motors turn left it's the first avenue on the left.
GPS 51.848889 -8.318242

LONGUEVILLE HOUSE

The O'Callaghan family
Mallow
North Cork
☎ **+353 (0) 22-47156**
🖰 **www.longuevillehouse.ie**
✉ **info@longuevillehouse.ie**

Relentless self-improvements and important developments mark the restless nature of Longueville, one of County Cork's great destinations.

Twenty years ago, when we first started to write about places to stay in Ireland, what impressed us about the best houses in Cork was the simple fact that the owners never rested on their laurels. Every winter brought new plans for improvement, sympathetic new developments. So, what's been going on at Longueville House, the O'Callaghan family's elegant, pretty-in-pink manor house, just outside Mallow? It would take a book to describe it all, but here's just a taste of what William and Aisling are up to: launching three new apple products from their orchard; an extended range of their artisan products from the walled garden; a fish smoking service for the day's catch for river anglers and sea fishermen who get lucky; fish cookery demonstrations by William O'Callaghan; a hamper service; management of 120 acres of ancient beech and oak woodland, and the planting of a further 120 acres... And that's just a taste of it, and in between times they look after you like you are a prince, and cook food that is fit for the gods!

● **OPEN:** all year, weekends only off season
● **ROOMS:** 20 rooms, all en suite
● **PRICE:** B&B €140-€180 in double room, €195-€260 in junior suite.

● **NOTES:** All major cards accepted. Dinner from 6.30pm, €40-€90. Recommended for vegetarians. Children welcome. No wheelchair facilities in rooms. Hotel will always open for groups of 20+

● **DIRECTIONS:**
5km from Mallow, travelling in direction of Killarney.
GPS 52.133515 -8.720934

47

NEWTOWN HOUSE

Georgie & Michael Penruddock
Kinsalebeg, Youghal
County Cork
📱 **+353 (0) 24-94304**
🖥 **www.stayatnewtown.com**
📧 **info@stayatnewtown.com**

"We were charmed!", says Caroline Hennessy of the charms of the beautiful Newtown House.

Something new

We were charmed. Charmed before we ever arrived by Georgie Penruddock's warmth on the phone, and her offer to babysit Little Missy if we wanted to go out for dinner. Charmed when we saw the breathtaking location – Newtown House is on the very, very edge of the Blackwater Estuary, directly across from Youghal – and charmed by our bright, graciously proportioned bedroom. From lolling in the roll-top bath-with-a-view, to relaxing with books in front of the drawing room fire and waking to the rapid whistle of the curlews as they skimmed across the estuary, our stay, although brief, felt like a true time out. Homegrown tomatoes, autumn raspberries and spicy myrtle berries, all gathered from the potager-style raised beds in the courtyard outside, featured at breakfast, along with just-arrived newspapers, entertaining conversation and tips on house refurbishment. We left feeling rested and revived precisely because of where we stayed, and who we stayed with. A retreat from the hurly burly of life.

- **OPEN:** All year
- **ROOMS:** Two double rooms, both en suite
- **PRICE:** B&B €65 per person sharing, €100 single occupancy

- **NOTES:** No credit cards. Limited wheelchair access. Picnics and light suppers by arrangement.

- **DIRECTIONS:**
From the village of Piltown, turn right to Ferrypoint. Proceed 0.7miles and the entrance is on the right. GPS 51.9584 -7.8231

PARADISO ROOMS

Denis Cotter
16 Lancaster Quay
Cork, County Cork
☎ **+353 (0) 21-427 7939**
🖰 **www.cafeparadiso.ie**
✉ **info@cafeparadiso.ie**

Café Paradiso and the Paradiso Rooms are a place like no other, elegantly simple spaces that enjoy a calming, quieting zen nature.

"I would happily eat in this restaurant every week!" is how Eamon Barrett of The Bridgestone Guides described the pleasures of Denis Cotter's unique vegetarian cooking, after staying in Cork, in the Paradiso Rooms, for a few days. In typical Cotter fashion, the Paradiso Rooms may be a restaurant with rooms – an r'n'r – but they are unlike any other r'n'r you have ever stayed at. The style is simpler, more colourful, an echo of the cookery style in Café Paradiso itself, where less somehow magically always seems to add up to more. They are wonderfully luxurious, but not in the way in which others concoct luxury – which just means adding in more and more. Instead they are lean, spacious, with everything well-chosen, from the bottled water to the CDs, the bathrooms to the bed linen. And it's wonderful to feel so close to the centre of the city, and what a splendid city Cork is: Dublin can feel parochial by comparison. And then, of course, there is the promise of dinner, no more than a stair's length away...

● **OPEN:** All year, except Christmas
● **ROOMS:** Two double rooms, all en suite
● **PRICE:** B&B and dinner €100 per person, sharing, Tue-Sat. €150 two nights + 1 dinner.

● **NOTES:** Visa, Mastercard.
Dinner, bed and breakfast packages always available. Breakfast menu also served in Cafe Paradiso restaurant. No wheelchair access.

● **DIRECTIONS:**
Opposite the Lancaster Lodge, on the right-hand side of the road, as you head west.

PIER HOUSE

Ann & Pat Hegarty
Pier Road
Kinsale, West Cork

📱 **+353 (0) 21-477 4475**
🖥 **www.pierhousekinsale.com**
✉ **pierhouseaccom@eircom.net**

It can be a heart-breaking experience, checking out of Ann and Pat's wonderful Pier House. You won't want to leave, and you will want to return.

When you get to know Kinsale as well as we do, having visited it and stayed here on numerous occasions over the last 20 years, you can forget the immense impact this pretty town wields on the first-time visitor.
A couple of years back, we were touring with the English writer Howard Jacobson – winner of the 2010 Man Booker prize! – and scooted straight down to Kinsale after picking Howard up from the airport. After about two minutes walking around the town, Howard confided that he wanted to get a little place in Kinsale, where he could write, and read, and chill out. Two minutes! Blimey! You too will experience this "I don't want to go home!" emotion, but even more strongly should you choose to stay in Ann Hegarty's brilliant Pier House. For a start, it's bang-smack in the centre of town, yet hidden by walls and hedges. Secondly, Mrs Hegarty is such a fine hostess, and looks after guests so well in her lovely house, that when it's time to go, you will likely blub. You won't be the first, or the last.

● **OPEN:** All year, except Christmas
● **ROOMS:** Nine rooms, all en suite
● **PRICE:** €120-€150 per room, including breakfast. Single €100-€140

● **NOTES:**
Visa, Mastercard, Laser. No wheelchair access. No dinner. One secure parking space, otherwise public carpark right next door.

● **DIRECTIONS:**
Coming from Cork, take first left at SuperValu, left at the tourist office, 50m down on right-hand side.

ROCK COTTAGE

Barbara Klotzer
Barnatonicane
Schull, West Cork
📱 **+353 (0) 28-35538**
🖥 **www.rockcottage.ie**
📠 **rockcottage@eircom.net**

A simply magical place, that is what Barbara Klotzer's Rock Cottage is. Everyone who stays here is ever enchanted by this West Cork star.

"What a great place it is!", our editor Eamon Barrett wrote about Barbara Klotzer's lovely, slate-covered lodge, just off the Goleen road in deepest West Cork. "There is just something magical about Rock Cottage." Well, Eamon is unquestionably right about this marvellous house, but what explains the magic? Great cooking, great housekeeping, calm comfort, a blissful retreat, a sublime location, that's what. Put all of these elements together with Ms Klotzer's ability to attend meticulously to every detail, and you have the magic. And we all need some magic in our lives: it was the late, great Richard Olney – the greatest food writer ever – who said to us once, as we enjoyed lunch at his place in Provence: "I believe in magic", when we asked him what captivated him about food, cooking and wine. When you find yourself enjoying dinner in Rock Cottage, after one of those beautiful days exploring West Cork when the sun shines, and the sea gleams, and time stands still, then you'll know what Olney meant.

- **OPEN:** All year
- **ROOMS:** Three en suite rooms & self-catering cottage
- **PRICE:** B&B €70 per person sharing. Single supplement €30

- **NOTES:** Visa, Mastercard. Dinner, 7.30pm, book 24hrs ahead, €50, set menu. BYO. Children over 10yrs.

- **DIRECTIONS:**
At Toormore turn right onto the R591 towards Durrus. After 2.4km you will see their sign on the left. GPS 51.545 -9.634722

ROLF'S COUNTRY HOUSE

Johannes & Frederike Haffner
Baltimore Hill
Baltimore, West Cork
📱 **+353 (0) 28-20289**
🖰 **www.rolfscountryhouse.eu**
🖾 **info@rolfscountryhouse.eu**

Rolf's is one of the real West Cork sports of nature, one of those special family institutions that exceed all your expectations. And then some...

Rolf's has come a long way from its early days when it operated primarily as a hostel, and today the accommodation, whilst still simple, is simply lovely: comfortable, cloistered, calm, a beautiful place in which to find yourself at any time of the year. Happily, the rooms are just as much fun as the cooking in their cosy restaurant, where the true strength is to be found in the mittel European specialities that Johannes really savours, such as their stroganoff, for instance, which is as good as you will get anywhere in Europe.

But aside from the comfort, the charm and the spot-on cooking, it is the energy and humour of Johannes and Frederike – and they are witty, droll, animated people – that animates Rolf's and gives it both character and soulfulness, making it a place loved by travellers and, crucially, beloved by locals: Rolf's isn't just for tourists, the locals eat here. It really is a smashing place, whether you are down in Baltimore for the boating, or just wending your way pleasurably through wonderful West Cork.

● **OPEN:** All year, except Christmas
● **ROOMS:** 14 rooms, all en suite
● **PRICE:** €40-€50 per person sharing, including continental breakfast.

● **NOTES:** Visa, Mastercard, Laser. No wheelchair access. Holiday cottages also available. Restaurant open 12.30pm-2.30pm, 6pm-9pm (9.30pm in summer)

● **DIRECTIONS:**
On the way to Baltimore just before village turn sharp left and follow signs, approx 200m up the hill.
GPS 51.480556 -9.367779

WITH GREAT BREAKFASTS

1
ARIEL HOUSE
COUNTY DUBLIN

2
BROOK'S HOTEL
COUNTY DUBLIN

3
FORTVIEW HOUSE
COUNTY CORK

4
THE HERON'S REST
COUNTY GALWAY

5
LOUGH BISHOP HOUSE
COUNTY WESTMEATH

6
NEWTOWN HOUSE
COUNTY CORK

7
NUMBER 31
COUNTY DUBLIN

8
SHEEDY'S
COUNTY CLARE

9
SHELBURNE LODGE
COUNTY KERRY

10
STELLA MARIS
COUNTY MAYO

SEA VIEW HOUSE HOTEL

Kathleen O'Sullivan
Ballylickey
Bantry, West Cork
📱 **+353 (0) 27-50462**
🖥 **www.seaviewhousehotel.com**
📧 **info@seaviewhousehotel.com**

One of the classic hotels of Ireland, Kathleen O'Sullivan's Sea View House is mature, calm, correct and eternally enjoyable, a paragon of virtue.

Writing about the fashion for trans-global fusion cooking which is sweeping the world, the great Ed Behr in *The Art of Eating*, writes that "The novelty often overwhelms anyone's judgements about what works and what doesn't... some people love a dish and some hate it, and then where are you, the potential customer?" If anything, the same problem is overwhelming traditional ideas and values of hospitality, with so many smart hotels today where the staff have so much attitude that you want to give them a slap, instead of a tip. But you will have no such problem in Kathleen O'Sullivan's truly excellent Victorian manor hotel, Sea View. Ms O'Sullivan is old school: correct cooking; correct service; correct design; correct housekeeping, and the pleasures to be derived from her didactic approach are myriad. This is hotel keeping of the old school, the good school, and it explains why so many customers regard Sea View as one of their favourite places to stay: the customer gets exactly what the customer wants.

● **OPEN:** mid Mar-mid Nov
● **ROOMS:** 25 rooms
● **PRICE:** B&B €120-€165 per room

● **NOTES:** All major cards accepted. Dinner in restaurant 6.45pm, Sun lunch (from Easter Sun) and lounge food daily. Dinner €35-€45. Wheelchair access. Secure parking. Pet friendly.

● **DIRECTIONS:**
On the N71 from Cork, 5km from Bantry and 13km from Glengarriff.
GPS 51.704722 -9.437222

TRAVARA LODGE

Brendan Murphy & Richard May
Courtmacsherry
West Cork
📱 **+353 (0) 23-884 6493**
🖱 **www.travaralodge.com**
📖 **travaralodge@eircom.net**

Brendan and Richard run a smashing show at the simple but engaging Travara Lodge. Good humour mixes with good cooking in this lovely address.

We get mails from Richard May every so often, and as we read them, we roar with laughter, we roar loudly with laughter, for this man is one of the most amusing people we have ever met. He's not just funny: he is also modest. "Comfortable bed plus excellent breakfast" is how Richard and Brendan describe their sea-facing guest house in pretty Courtmac (as the locals call it). But that is too modest by half. Travara is a smashing house: comfortable, relaxing, with superb cooking to ease you into another day of not doing too much. Add in Brendan's great cooking to the mix, and you have a simple, dreamy, B&B in a beautiful West Cork village. Food lovers should note that Brendan bakes for the local Friday market, and that you can also buy his wonderful cooking at The Chessboard in the village on Saturday mornings. What you need to know is that Mr Murphy is actually a chef and baker of quite some renown, known nationally for his amazing wedding cakes, so you had better get there early!

- ● **OPEN:** All year, except Nov
- ● **ROOMS:** Six rooms, all en suite
- ● **PRICE:** B&B €80 per double room,

● **NOTES:**
Visa, Mastercard, Laser
No dinner. Limited wheelchair access.

● **DIRECTIONS:**
The house overlooks the bay, in the centre of the village.

CASTLE MURRAY HOUSE HOTEL

Marguerite Howley
Dunkineely, County Donegal
📱 **+353 (0) 74-973 7022**
🖰 www.castlemurray.com
📧 info@castlemurray.com

They make you welcome in Castle Murray, they make you smile, and they do their best to make you happy. And they've been doing it for 20 years.

Consistency, consistency, consistency. That's what you get in Marguerite Howley's Castle Murray House, and that's why Castle Murray House has been in the *Bridgestone Guides* ever since our first book, back in 1991. That's a long and successful tenure in Irish hospitality. Part of their success is explained by the fact that Remy Dupuy has been in the kitchen since 1994, cooking house classics such as prawns and monkfish in garlic butter, tartare of Inver sea trout with blinis, or ravioli of Donegal crab. And, since 1991, we have been writing that the views from the dining room are amongst the most captivating in the entire county, and this is a county that does views everywhichway. The rooms are simple and comfortable, the hospitality genuine and fetching. "Peopled by warm, charming staff who made us welcome, made us laugh, and made us some truly excellent food", as a correspondent noted in a brilliant piece of analysis which explains how this house works: they make you welcome, make you happy.

● **OPEN:** All year, except Xmas and mid Jan-mid Feb. Closed Mon & Tues except Jul & Aug. Oct-Dec weekends
● **ROOMS:** Ten rooms
● **PRICE:** B&B €40-€55 per person sharing. Single €50-€65

● **NOTES:** Visa, Mastercard, Laser. Restaurant open 6.30pm-9.30pm Mon-Sat; 1.30pm-3.30pm, 6.30pm-8.30pm Sun; Dinner €45 No wheelchair access. Pet friendly.

● **DIRECTIONS:**
Castle Murray is signposted just west of Dunkineely.

LINSFORT CASTLE

Alan Rooks
Buncrana, County Donegal
📱 +353 (0) 87 9677244
📱 +353 (0) 74-936 3148
🖰 www.linsfortcastle.com
📧 booking@linsfortcastle.com

Linsfort Castle sounds
grand, but Alan Rooks'
house is the most modest,
unpretentious castle.

We weren't thinking of Linsfort Castle as a potential
Bridgestone entrant when we travelled 'oop north to
Inishowen for a week in August 2010. A friend organ-
ised it, and so we turned up and said hello to Alan and
Brid and Riley the dog, and settled ourselves in, and
walked down to the little deserted beach just down
from the house, and then headed into Buncrana for
dinner and came home and slept like logs. And then
we had Alan's special porridge and one of the best
cooked breakfasts we have had in yonks in the lovely
breakfast room with its traditional fireplace and suddenly everyone was saying "Isn't Linsfort just terrific!",
and everyone was agreeing, and that was before Alan
cooked dinner for us one night and that dinner was fantastic and suddenly we are having the best time ever in
Linsfort and we're saying to each other, "Isn't this the
sort of place that Bridgestone is all about?" and everyone is agreeing, and so here it is: Linsfort Castle in the
Bridgestone 100 Best Places to Stay. We're smitten.

● **OPEN:** All year
● **ROOMS:** Five rooms, three bathrooms
● **PRICE:** B&B €35 per person

● **NOTES:** No credit cards. Dinner by arrangement.
Ideal for small groups or families. Comfortable lounge
with library. Sun terrace. Recommended for Vegetarians.
Pet friendly. No wheelchair access.

● **DIRECTIONS:**
Turn left over the bridge on northside of Buncrana. Follow Inishowen 100 and Dunree road for 4km until road
forks. Take left fork. GPS 55.17171 -7.50103

McGRORY'S

Anne, John & Neil McGrory
Culdaff
County Donegal
📞 +353 (0) 74-937 9104
🖐 www.mcgrorys.ie
✉ info@mcgrorys.ie

Inishowen was the Costa del Sol for holidaymakers from Scotland sixty year ago. Sixty years on, and it's still magic, and so is mighty McGrory's.

The Inishowen legend that is the mighty McGrory's powers on through the years, with siblings Anne, John and Neil ladling out the hospitality as to the Donegal manner born. There is something so very generous about this trio as they go about their business: managing the bar, managing the restaurant and the rooms, managing the music and the gigs, so generous with their time, their energy, their knowledge and experience, that it animates the entire place. The music sessions held here are the stuff of legend, of course, but McGrory's is special whether you can pick with a plectrum or pluck a pizzicato, or whether your speciality is listening to other people doing just that. Establishing a destination address in such a remote, northerly place is an heroic act, but the McGrorys are wise people: they have developed slowly, organically, patiently, and they exude the culture of their area with delightful charm. This is a magical peninsula, and McGrory's your magical lodging.

● **OPEN:** All year, except Mon & Tue off season.
● **ROOMS:** 17 rooms
● **PRICE:** B&B €89-€109 per double room, €59-€69 per single room

● **NOTES:** Visa, Master, Laser, Amex. Food served in bar and restaurant Mon-Sun. Bar food served all year 12.30pm-9pm. Restaurant hours can vary according to season, so it is wise to check. Wheelchair access.

● **DIRECTIONS:**
On the main R238 between Moville and Malin Head.
GPS 55.286301 -7.165618

THE MILL

Derek & Susan Alcorn
Figart, Dunfanaghy,
County Donegal
☏ +353 (0) 74-913 6985
🖱 www.themillrestaurant.com
✉ themillrestaurant@oceanfree.net

A decade of success, and hard work, for Derek and Susan has made The Mill a star of County Donegal.

Derek and Susan Alcorn's The Mill debuted in the Bridgestones back in 2001, having hit the ground running with a restaurant with rooms – an r'n' r – offer that was perfectly minted, and fully formed, right from the off. Since then, things have simply gotten better in this most lovely house. The hospitality is confident and calm, and Mr Alcorn's cooking just gets better and better, offering some of the best food in the North West: salad of chorizo, broad beans, olives and soft boiled egg; leek and asparagus risotto; Horn Head lamb with basil mash; chocolate torte with chocolate and thyme ice cream. Derek Alcorn is a singular cook, devoted to local foods to which he shows the ultimate respect, and he has always encouraged a great team of local talent to work alongside him.

The setting of the house, by the calm, mysterious New Lake on the road west out of Dunfanaghy, is blissful, and the design style of The Mill has never needed to be altered since they opened. A decade of sheer brilliance.

● **OPEN:** Easter to Hallowe'en, weekends off season
● **ROOMS:** Six rooms
● **PRICE:** €50 per person sharing, €75 single.

● **NOTES:** Visa, Mastercard, Laser, Amex.
No wheelchair access.
Recommended for children.

● **DIRECTIONS:**
Dunfanaghy is at the very tip of the country, coming up to Horn Head. From L'Kenny take the N56 through Dunfanaghy. The Mill is 1km past the village on right.
GPS 55.176856 -7.980311

MOORFIELD LODGE

Lin Crossle
Letterkenny, Ramelton
County Donegal
📱 **+353 (0) 74-915 2655**
🖥 **www.moorfieldlodge.com**
📧 **info@gortnadihalodge.com**

A great new arrival in County Donegal, Moorfield Lodge is a vivid, modern house, just oozing great hospitality.

Something new

Lin and Bobby Crossle's stunning boutique B&B raises the bar for levels of contemporary comfort in Donegal. Moorfield has three suites – The Spa; the Bayview and the Classic – and we guess that if you are in Ramelton for a special occasion then you're going to want to go the whole hog and book the Spa suite because, CS Lewis-style, the spa room is hidden in a wardrobe which opens out, revealing a luxurious space where you could while away half a day, no problem. A WOW! room. Ms Crossle has hospitality in her bones, and a love of good food. Her breakfast granola is superb, as is the strawberry and blueberry crêpe. "We try to bend to please the guest in every way possible. We are doing this for the love of it," she explains. And this luxury would be nothing without the friendliness which the couple exude, and it is this charm that animates Moorfield. The Crossles spent a long time looking for just the right property to develop as a B&B, but even if they ran a Nissen hut, you would stay with them.

● **OPEN:** All year except Christmas
● **ROOMS:** Three suites
● **PRICE:** B&B €80 for the Classic, €120 for the Bayview, €135 for the Spa Suite

● **NOTES:** No credit cards. Not suitable for children. Wheelchair access with assistance - please ask.

● **DIRECTIONS:**
From Letterkenny's Polestar roundabout head toward Ramelton. 2 miles past the Silver Tassie Hotel, pass X-sign, squiggly road sign then turn left at the next cross. GPS 55.0094833 -7.658445

RATHMULLAN HOUSE

The Wheeler family
Lough Swilly, Rathmullan
County Donegal
📱 **+353 (0) 74-915 8188**
🖱 **www.rathmullanhouse.com**
📩 **info@rathmullanhouse.com**

The Wheeler family's Rathmullan House offers one of the most seductive, sustainable, authentic country house experiences.

My goodness but Rathmullan House was buzzing on the evening when the McKenna family took the Lough Swilly ferry over from Buncrana to have dinner in this beautiful, elegant country house. Loads of children outside playing in the grounds and firing around on bicycles. Happy punters and diners and groups and friends milling and chatting inside the house from all over the country and further field – from all over the globe, in fact. Rathmullan was offering proof, once again, if proof were needed, that all you need to survive a recession is to be a world-class destination. Kelan McMichael's cooking at Rathmullan is understated and serene, and is just the right fit for the calmness of the Weeping Elm restaurant: Burtonport razor clams with Donegal rapeseed oil; Lough Swilly halibut with steamed samphire; Fermanagh lamb with minted pea purée; free-range chicken with garden chard. The produce of their gardens is used to full effect, and the Wheeler family work hard to make everyone happy.

● **OPEN:** Open all year, apart from mid Jan-mid Feb and closed mid week Nov & Dec
● **ROOMS:** 34 rooms
● **PRICE:** €85-€140 per person

● **NOTES:** Visa, Laser, Mastercard, Amex. Wheelchair access. Swimming pool. Pet friendly. Family rooms. Loc8 code CGG W7R6

● **DIRECTIONS:**
In Rathmullan, turn left at the Mace shop. Go north through the village, past the Blue Church, turn right at black gates. GPS 55.09871 -7.53443

ABERDEEN LODGE

Pat Halpin
53-55 Park Avenue, Ballsbridge
Dublin 4
📞 **+353 (0) 1-283 8155**
🖥 www.halpinsprivatehotels.com
✉ reservations@halpinsprivatehotels.com

Pat and Anne's Aberdeen
Lodge is the quintessential
Ballsbridge townhouse: calm;
gracious; sophisticated; chic.

Up to Dublin for a family party, and where else would
you be staying other than Aberdeen Lodge? They were
hosting a small, private wedding on the evening of the
day we arrived, and we all thought: what a great place for
a reception, in the lovely dining room, with the patio and
garden to enjoy. Why? Because everyone who stays here
is always so well looked-after. It's tangible. It's people
going the extra distance in terms of service, professionalism, polish. It's people chasing perfection in their work,
led from the front by Pat and Anne. It shows in the quality of the breakfast. In the quality of the tea and home-
made biscuits when you arrive. It shows in the way in
which everything is done properly. Not proper in some
snobbish way, but properly because that is the best way
to do things, the way that gives most delight. So, turn up
at this handsome Victorian house in a quiet, leafy Sandy-
mount avenue, and experience for yourself the delight in
having things done properly. We had, as usual, a fantastic
time, and we'll be back.

● **OPEN:** All year
● **ROOMS:** 17 rooms, including two suites
● **PRICE:** €65-€90 per person sharing, €99-€120
single

● **NOTES:** All major cards accepted. Light 'drawing
room' menu, €8-€15 per course, extensive wine list.
Parking. Wheelchair access. Not suitable for children
under 7yrs. Concierge Service.

● **DIRECTIONS:**
Just down from the Sydney Parade DART station.
GPS 53.325017 -6.213247

ARIEL HOUSE

Deirdre McDonald
50-54 Lansdowne Road
Dublin 4
☎ **+353 (0) 1-668 5512**
✉ **reservations@ariel-house.net**
🖰 **www.ariel-house.net**

Ariel is a classic Dublin townhouse that leaves no one unconvinced of its capacious merits.

Something new

Here's how our mate Eugene describes Ariel House, on leafy Lansdowne Road: "I discovered Ariel House early this year and it has become a home from home for us when we stay in Dublin. It has no restaurant but the staff and standards and especially the welcome are outstanding. Lovely location, family owned, comfortable rooms, afternoon tea on arrival, and the breakfast next morning is superb. A cold buffet display of the usual plus lovely cheese and pickles, thick sliced home baked ham and mustard, smoked salmon and the hot dishes are all wonderful. I would gladly drive to Dublin just to have their poached eggs on home-made toasted brown bread with smoked salmon and the lightest lemon butter sauce! My wife still raves about the French toast with berries. I know you are smothered with recommendations in Bridgestone, but to us, Ariel House is wonderful. The general manager Deirdre McDonald epitomises to us what Irish charm and professionalism is all about." That will do nicely.

● **OPEN:** All year, except Christmas
● **ROOMS:** 37 rooms, all ensuite
● **PRICE:** B&B from €79 per room

● **NOTES:**
Visa, Mastercard, Laser, Amex. Facilities for wheelchair customers. Complementary car parking. Afternoon tea served 2pm-5pm daily. Children welcome.

● **DIRECTIONS:**
Right beside the Aviva stadium.
GPS 53.334153 -6.231103

BROOK'S HOTEL

Claire Leahy
Drury Street
Dublin 2
📱 **+353 (0) 1-670 4000**
🖱 www.brookshotel.ie
📧 reservations@brookshotel.ie

Every member of staff in Brook's Hotel is a star, everyone over-delivers, which is why it is simply the best hotel in Dublin.

When we have written about Brook's Hotel in the past, we have tended to concentrate on the extraordinary standards of service that the hotel's staff deliver for guests. This has led us to overlook the stellar quality of the cooking from chef Patrick McLarnon and his team, so it's about time that we put that right: the food in Brook's is ace, a sympathetic, modest modern Irish cuisine that is beautifully achieved, and which has a sense of true, holistic goodness to it. Taste these flavours and you won't be surprised to hear that Mr McLarnon isn't just a cook, he is also a man who has an allotment in order to grow his own vegetables, and his food has the earthy qualities you would expect from a man who knows the true value of pure, undiluted flavours, whether he is making a navarin of Irish lamb, or baking the most wonderful Xmas cake, or ensuring that every element of an Irish breakfast is as fine as it can be. Pastry chef Emily Kay is also a star-in-waiting, another key player in the very best hotel in Dublin city.

● **OPEN:** All year including Christmas
● **ROOMS:** 98 bedrooms, including three suites
● **PRICE:** €80-€90 standard double, per person sharing, single supplement €65

● **NOTES:** Visa, Mastercard, Amex. Restaurant open breakfast & dinner. Bar serves food 10am-6pm, & 6pm-10pm. Fitness suite. Pillow menu. Wi-Fi.

● **DIRECTIONS:**
Drury Street is parallel to Grafton St, between Grafton St and Sth Gt George's St, in the centre of Dublin.
GPS 53.3421615 -6.2634513

NUMBER 31

Noel Conroy
31 Lower Leeson Street
Dublin 4

☎ + 353 (0) 1-676 5011
🖰 www.number31.ie
✉ number31@iol.ie

Turn up at No 31 looking forward to the design of this iconic masterpiece and you'll soon find out every other detail of the house is just as stellar.

Noel Conroy, owner of the iconic No 31, brought in the brilliant Garret O'Hagan of O'Hagan Design to do some work on the interiors of the Georgian house that is one part of this landmark Dublin destination. The result has been to create rooms that are as equally classic as the rooms in the modern mews of the house. Deep greys and browns are restful and demure, modern sofas and chaises-longues bullet-point the rooms with drama, making for spaces to linger and lounge. Brilliant work. Whilst the great design alone would make No 31 a dream destination, the totality of the house is completed by one of the very best breakfasts cooked in the city. Cooke's Bakery bread makes the best toast, cereals and fruits are sublime, scrambled eggs with smoked salmon achieves perfection, and the presentation of the table is always simply outstanding. The effect of this aesthetic paragon is to simply lift the spirits first thing in the morning, and it confirms No 31 as a vital Dublin destination. An icon.

● **OPEN:** all year, including Christmas
● **ROOMS:** 21 bedrooms
● **PRICE:** €140-€220 per room

● **NOTES:**
Visa, Mastercard, Laser, Amex
No wheelchair access

● **DIRECTIONS:**
At the upper end of Lower Leeson Street, near the corner with Fitzwilliam Place, in the centre of Dublin.

PEMBROKE HOUSE

Fiona Teehan
90 Pembroke Road, Ballsbridge
Dublin 4
📱 +353 (0) 1-660 0277
🖰 www.pembroketownhouse.ie
✉ info@pembroketownhouse.ie

Pembroke House is a real feel-good destination, and Fiona Teehan and her team are the hardest working crew in the city, hopelessly devoted to you.

A beautiful location on tree-lined Pembroke Road is just one of the major assets of Fiona Teehan's Pembroke House, though its real secret is the fact that the exceptionally fine staff match the fine location, and they also bring alive the grandeur of the house itself. The bedrooms are calming and very, very comfortable, stylish without being slaves to design, so their focus is on a comfort that makes you feel very good indeed, especially when the staff arrive with some tea and hand-made biscuits to calm the weary traveller. That feel-good factor is an important element of Pembroke House, because it's one of those elements that is hard to capture, hard to conjure, hard to create. But when someone gets it – as Ms Teehan and her team do – then it means that the guest is a very happy camper indeed. The public rooms are cosy and clubbable, and a good place in which to help yourself to a drink from the bar, and the staff look after you properly, in that waggish Dublin way which is so fine.

● **OPEN:** All year, except two weeks at Christmas
● **ROOMS:** 48 rooms, all en suite (incl seven suites)
● **PRICE:** from €99 per person

● **NOTES:** All major cards accepted. Parking complimentary to residents. Car park entrance is on Baggot Lane. Wheelchair access.

● **DIRECTIONS:**
Pembroke Road is at the Southern end of Upper Baggot Street. Pembroke Townhouse faces Raglan Road with large lanterns on each side of the front door.
GPS 53.332476 -6.23806

ANGLER'S RETURN

Lynn Hill
Toombeola, Roundstone
Connemara, County Galway
📞 **+ 353 (0) 95-31091**
🖱 **www.anglersreturn.com**
✉ **info@anglersreturn.com**

It's more than just anglers who return to Lynn Hill's beautiful Roundstone cottage, an aesthetic Connemara treasure, always picture postcard perfect.

Lynn Hill's Angler's Return is a picture postcard pretty house, by the side of the lake out in Toombeola, and you could be won over in its favour simply by a first glance at its flower-bedecked finery and its sublime location. But there is more to the Return than just the facade of prettiness. Ms Hill marries an ethos to her aesthetic which means that the Angler's Return is a house where people feel at ease, left alone to enjoy the garden, the house and the river. And behind the pretty facade, Lynn has worked hard to create the most aesthetically pleasing place in which to relax and recuperate. This also means delivering the best quality cooking, and doing so in such a way that expresses her own determination to achieve purity and simplicity. This is one of those houses that feels quintessentially Connemara – a place apart, superbly self contained, a welcoming ship of delights in one of the most austere yet lovable landscapes in the entire country. Expect to be captivated by a house that makes time stand still.

● **OPEN:** open Feb-Nov
● **ROOMS:** five rooms, one en suite, four other rooms share two adjacent bathrooms
● **PRICE:** from €90 per double room

● **NOTES:**
No credit cards.
Not suitable for children under 8 years, babes in arms welcome.

● **DIRECTIONS:**
Four miles, on the Galway side, of Roundstone.

BALLYNAHINCH CASTLE

Patrick O'Flaherty
Ballinafad, Recess, Connemara
County Galway

📞 **+353 (0) 95-31006**
🖱 **www.ballynahinch-castle.com**
📧 **bhinch@iol.ie**

Ballynahinch Castle is a star destination, a place where hospitality, service and cooking synthesise in calm perfection.

They understand hospitality at Ballynahinch, they understand how to draw down, how to trigger, the archetypal images and memories in your mind about what hospitality means. The fire is always lit as you come through the door; the bar always has a gregarious mix of drinkers; the dining room says elegance, romance, the charm of nature outside the window captured for your gaze; the food on the plate says delight and satisfaction, the wine in the glass says delightful good times. The team are so good because they are confident. Patrick O'Flaherty knows his business back to front, whilst chef Xin Sun has been powering the kitchen forward over the last couple of years, concocting a fine modern cuisine that is a thrill to eat thanks to a host of unexpected details: St Tola goat's cheese with an unusual aduki bean parfait; pork fillet wrapped in McGeough's air-dried ham; a chilli risotto with wild turbot; a note of lemongrass in the saffron and cream sauce for panache of seafood. A peachy, perfect place.

● **OPEN:** All year, except Feb and Christmas
● **ROOMS:** 40 rooms, including three suites
● **PRICE:** €80-€245 per person sharing, single supplement €45

● **NOTES:** All major cards accepted. Dinner in restaurant, €60. No wheelchair access. Private fishery, walking routes and hikes.

● **DIRECTIONS:**
From Galway, take signs for Clifden (N59). At Recess you will begin to see their signs.
GPS 53.4602166 -9.86311666

CONNEMARA COAST HOTEL

Ann Downey (General Manager)
Furbo, Galway
County Galway
+ 353 (0) 91-592108
www.connemaracoast.ie
info@connemaracoast.ie

Hotelier Charles Synnott runs hotels on both the east and west coasts, and runs both of them superbly well, epitomising the art of hotelkeeping.

Charles Synnott understands the business of running hotels. Mr Synnott understands that to run an hotel, you need to be an hotelier, that most noble, and difficult, of callings. In fact, he runs two hotels in this book, and it is their difference, and their distinctiveness, that appeals to us. Brook's Hotel in Dublin is the only Dublin hotel in this book, and it is there because it is a quintessential city hotel. But the Connemara Coast is a quintessential resort hotel, a place to escape to from the city, a place to enjoy sea air, good food, a beautiful art collection, along with excellent service from a crack team who know their work inside out, led by manager Ann Downey. The CCH is a place to relax, and the staff are able to create the Ocean Liner effect perfectly: when you stay here, you are away from it all, the workaday world has departed, and you and your family are on vacation. To create this feeling is the true art of the hotelier, and you will rarely see it practised better than it is practised in this West Coast getaway.

● **OPEN:** open all year except Christmas
● **ROOMS:** 141 rooms, standard, superior & executive
● **PRICE:** €89-€125 per person sharing. Supplements (around €50) apply to superior rooms and suites.

● **NOTES:** Visa, Mastercard, Laser, Amex. Mid-week offers available. Wheelchair access. Two restaurants, cocktail bar and pub.

● **DIRECTIONS:**
From Galway, follow signs for Clifden and Oughterard. The Connemara Coast is on this road on the left, in the village of Furbo, just after Barna.

DELPHI LODGE

Peter Mantle
Leenane, Connemara
County Galway

📱 **+353 (0) 95-42222**
🖥 **www.delphilodge.ie**
✉ **res@delphilodge.ie**

It's not just the many charms of Delphi Lodge that make it what it is. It's also that they know what they don't want to be.

The reason why Peter Mantle's country house and estate is world renowned is not just because of what it is, but also because of what it is not. Yes, it is renowned for being a beautiful house in one of the most beautiful places in Ireland – if not the world. And yes it is beloved of fishermen hoping for a salmon, and it is beloved of food lovers who relish Cliodna Prendergasts's cooking, whilst wine buffs can simply lose themselves in the incredible selection of wines on the list. But these alone don't explain Delphi's renown. No, equally important to its substantial assets are the fact that Delphi in no way tries to be an hotel, or to ape hotel-style service. It has stubbornly and determinedly set its face against the modern blandness that people think of as luxury. So instead it is quaint, a place that is comfortable with itself, which means you will be comfortable with it too. In Delphi, they know what they can do best, and the best is what they do. It seems a simple thing, but it demands calm confidence.

● **OPEN:** Mar-Sep (house parties 18+ off season)
● **ROOMS:** 12 rooms, all en suite (seven with lake view)
● **PRICE:** from €99 per person. Single suppl. €33.

● **NOTES:** Visa & Mastercard. Dinner, 8pm, communal table €49. Wheelchair accessible, but not fully disabled-friendly. Flyfishing. Billiards room. Not suitable for young children.

● **DIRECTIONS:**
12km northwest of Leenane on the Louisburgh road. In woods on left about half mile after the Adventure Spa. GPS 53.631916 -9.747190

DEVON DELL

Berna Kelly
47 Devon Park
Lower Salthill, Galway city
📞 **+353 (0) 91-528306**
🖱 **www.devondell.com**
✉ **devondel@iol.ie**

Every morning Berna Kelly prepares breakfast as if it is a brand new creation being fashioned for the very first time. That's a Zen mind for you.

Devon Dell may be a simple house, set in a quiet cul-de-sac a short stroll from the centre of Galway, but it's precisely the kind of place that Galway does well: individual; aspirational, a bit naive, pure delight. In Berna Kelly's house, the housekeeping that you experience, the stellar standards of cooking, the thoughtfulness of the hospitality, are exactly the things that Galway citizens do the best. It's pure Galway, in the way that some places are pure West Cork. Hard to define, but you know it when you get it. And that is what you get in Devon Dell: pure Galway. Mrs Kelly has a beginner's mind, the true Zen mind, when it comes to cooking. Each morning, it is as if the breakfast has been fashioned with a beginner's mind, so everything seems newly minted, full of culinary possibilities, crafted with generosity and openness, and without cliché or rote. It is a marvellous performance, and it is created every morning with the fastidiousness of Zen, and the zeitgeist of Galway. The city spirit is here.

- ● **OPEN:** Mar-Oct
- ● **ROOMS:** 2 double rooms, 1 twin & 1 single, en suite
- ● **PRICE:** €45 per person sharing

- ● **NOTES:** No credit cards. No wheelchair access. No facilities for very young children. Street parking.

- ● **DIRECTIONS:**
Find Fr Griffin Rd, and follow to T-junction, where you take left into Lr Salthill Rd. After approx 500m, having passed two pubs, take first right. Go 100m to fork in road, take left and very sharp left into cul-de-sac.
GPS 53.265192 -9.073872

DOLPHIN BEACH

The Foyle family
Lower Sky Road, Clifden
Connemara, County Galway
☎ **+ 353 (0) 95-21204**
🖑 **www.dolphinbeachhouse.com**
✉ **stay@dolphinbeachhouse.com**

Dolphin Beach is a famously stylish destination. Here is Elizbeth Field's ode – no less, no less – to its many, varied and delightful charms.

"Dolphin Beach embodies all I would wish to have in a small hotel. Gorgeous views over the Atlantic Ocean, Slyne Head and Ballyconneely Bay; sparkling clear Western light and fresh breezes; relaxing peace and quiet; wonderful locally sourced food and inimitable Irish hospitality. The small details are all there: the comforting pot of tea and biscuits when you arrive; perfect beds with crisp linen; beautiful books to leaf through in the front room; home-made breads and jam. I love the spare, Scandinavian-inspired modern decor: lots of wood, lots of windows, rooms that open directly onto a patio. Clodagh Foyle has innkeeping in her blood and it shows. She effortlessly juggles a million household tasks and is always ready with a smile. A brief meander up Sky Road after a summer dinner gave us but the baaaah of sheep, the rustling of trees, the smell of honeysuckle and a drawn-out sunset over the water. This is the place I would choose to truly unwind." Ahhh, only in beautiful Connemara.

● **OPEN:** mid Feb-mid Nov
● **ROOMS:** Nine en suite rooms
● **PRICE:** €60-€85 per person sharing. Single supplement €20

● **NOTES:**
Dinner if booked in advance, €40. Visa, Mastercard, Laser. Limited wheelchair access. Loc8 Code is KLR-90-R66

● **DIRECTIONS:**
Take the Sky road out of Clifden, take the lower fork for 1 mile. It's the house on the sea side.
GPS 53.497778 -10.094722

THE HERON'S REST

Sorcha Mulloy
16a Longwalk, Spanish Arch
Galway, County Galway
📱 **+353 (0) 86-337 9343**
🖥 **www.theheronsrest.com**
✉ **theheronsrest@gmail.com**

Sorcha Mulloy's riverside B&B in the centre of Galway is magnificent, and has the country's most original breakfast.

We are in awe of Sorcha Mulloy. The way she does things is just not the way other people do things. She doesn't just do them differently; she does them better. She can conceptualise something others take for granted – breakfast, for instance – and her concept has all the things you don't expect from the first meal of the day. The Heron's Rest breakfast has Drama! Creativity! Originality! Start with pearl barley porridge with honeyed dates, try some slow-baked rhubarb French toast with toasted almonds, continue with saffron spiced smoked Galway mackerel with Burren greens, and you will know that you are in a breakfast place you have never visited before. Different, and better, and thrilling. And then there is a HR picnic basket for your day's travelling, and one of Sorcha's fish dinners to look forward to in the evening, with the fish delivered straight from the boats by Tommy Connolly. There isn't a better place to stay in Ireland. We're in awe of Sorcha Mulloy. You will be too.

● **OPEN:** May 1-Sept 30
● **ROOMS:** Three double rooms, two singles: double rooms en suite or private bath, single sharing bathroom.
● **PRICE:** €65-€70 per person sharing

● **NOTES:**
All major credit cards accepted. No wheelchair access. Street parking in front of house. Children welcome.

● **DIRECTIONS:**
Follow signs for East Galway and Docks. Turn left at Sheridan's and follow the road around to the right. Heron's Rest is facing the water.

INIS MEÁIN SUITES

Ruairí & Marie-Therese de Blacam
Inis Meáin, Aran Islands
County Galway
📱 **+ 353 (0) 86-826 6026**
🖐 **www.inismeain.com**
📫 **post@inismeain.com**

The hottest destination, created by the most dynamic young couple in Irish hospitality, the de Blácams of Inis Meain.

Ruairi and Marie-Therese de Blácam are the coolest cats on the island, and by that we don't just mean the island of Inis Meain, we actually mean the island of Ireland of which Inis Meain is a small, and very beautiful, part. Their suites and restaurant already enjoy a cult status amongst food lovers and travellers that few addresses ever achieve, never mind places that have actually only been open for a few seasons.
Their secret is simple: as a couple they are blessed with a shared aesthetic, and in many ways almost a shared intellect. They have fashioned something brand new – their gorgeous restaurant and four state-of-the-art suites. And yet, paradoxically, staying and eating here feels like you have come to a place that is ageless, and ancient, not someplace new and modish. This fusion of modernity and timelessness doesn't exist in many places and, along with Mr de Blacam's thunderously fine cooking, it makes for one of the great Irish hospitality experiences. Once in your lifetime, make it over to here.

● **OPEN:** April-Sept
● **ROOMS:** four large suites
● **PRICE:** B&B €250-€350 per person. Two-night stay minimum. Packages available.

● **NOTES:** Visa, Mastercard, Laser. Restaurant open for Dinner, main courses €16-€35.

● **DIRECTIONS:**
Take the ferry from Rossaveal, or plane from Inverin. You find the house in the middle of the island, pass the only pub on your right, take the next right, then look out for stone building 100m on your left.

74

KILMURVEY HOUSE

Treasa & Bertie Joyce
Kilmurvey Bay, Inis Mór
Aran Islands, County Galway
📱 +353 (0) 99-61218
📧 kilmurveyhouse@eircom.net
🖰 www.kilmurveyhouse.com

Have you ever met hosts who are as thoughtful as Treasa and Bertie Joyce of Kilmurvey House? They are the heart and soul of Aran, in every way.

As with so many – indeed virtually all! – of the people in this latest Bridgstone guide, Treasa Joyce of Kilmurvey House on Inis Mor has had a great season in 2010. How to explain this seemingly bewildering success in the face of such a serious recession in Ireland? Simple: when the going get tough, people opt for the tried and trusted. They return to the places where they know they will be looked after. They go back to the people whose reputations are founded on care, hospitality, and hard work. And you don't get better care, hospitality, or a more hard-working woman, than Treasa Joyce of Kilmurvey House. If you're crazy enough not to want to eat dinner here, then Bertie will drive you down to Kilronan. But you should really make the smart choice and opt to enjoy Treasa's dinners, for this lady is a skilful, loving cook, and her food brims with TLC. Breakfast is a treat, the rooms are lovely, the house is comfy, the beach is just down the road and Dun Aengus is just up the hill, and sure where else would you want to be!

● **OPEN:** 1 Apr-16 Oct
● **ROOMS:** 12 rooms, all en suite (seven family rooms)
● **PRICE:** €45-€50 per person sharing. Single €60-€65

● **NOTES:**
No wheelchair access. Dinner by arrangement only. Complimentary bus to Kilronan for dinner, or evening snack menu served in the house.

● **DIRECTIONS:**
The house is a further 7km from the ferry port. On arrival, take any one of the tour buses.

THE QUAY HOUSE

Paddy & Julia Foyle
Beach Road, Clifden
Connemara, County Galway
📞 **+353 (0) 95-21369**
🖰 **www.thequayhouse.com**
📧 **res@thequayhouse.com**

"That Foyle family is something else! Honestly, Irish hospitality at its best is unbeatable." So says Elizabeth Field.

We have written about Quay House for two decades, so here is our editor Elizabeth Field's reaction as a first-time visitor to Paddy and Julia Foyle's gorgeous house: "This place has tons of style: overstuffed sofas and chairs, walls chock-a-block with paintings and ornaments; plump pillows; meandering corridors. Our room on the third floor overlooked the quay. It was HUGE, with a canopy bed, comfortable seating, and I think a fireplace. Also a lovely old-fashioned large bathroom. The breakfast was outstanding: scrambled eggs with smoked salmon; porridge with berry compote; and all the fixings of the full Irish – something I really miss on the other side of the pond. The Foyles are absolutely dynamic: funny, warm, urbane and welcoming. It's a 3-minute walk to town, which is quite nice, as the town can get pretty crowded. So you feel like you're in your own private, rambling, wisteria-covered residence. I wouldn't want to stay anyplace else in Clifden." Liz will be back!

● **OPEN:** mid Mar-early Nov
● **ROOMS:** 14 en suite rooms, including rooms with kitchens
● **PRICE:** B&B from €75 per person sharing, €100-€120 single rate

● **NOTES:** Visa, Mastercard, Laser. No dinner. Wheelchair access. Street parking.

● **DIRECTIONS:**
The Quay House is down on the quays, past the small playground, and overlooking the harbour.
GPS 53.463525 -10.033264

76

RENYLE HOUSE

Ronnie Counihan
Renvyle, Connemara
County Galway
📞 **+353 (0) 95-43511**
🖱 **www.renvyle.com**
✉ **info@renvyle.com**

A coastal country house that is unlike any other address in Ireland, Renvyle marries great hospitality and food.

Ronnie Counihan and chef Tim O'Sullivan run one of Ireland's best destinations, out there on the westerly shores, in a house that is a place and a passion unto itself. It is hard to know who loves Renvyle more: McKenna adults? Or McKenna children? Guess we will have to just take another trip to this magical little universe and then argue the toss one more time. Mr O'Sullivan's cooking, in particular, is amongst the finest country house cooking anywhere in Europe, both hugely disciplined and yet enjoying a free-form energy that makes it seem as if he has just dreamt it all up. Don't make the mistake of thinking that what Renvyle offers is "hotel" food. It isn't: this is cutting-edge cooking from a master chef who is currently at the very height of his powers. Put that food in an energised dining room, and with an excellent pianist who even manages some Chopin, so do ask for a little mazurka as you sip your wine and relish dinner. Chopin seduced the piano: Renvyle will seduce you.

- **OPEN:** Feb-Nov. Open for Christmas.
- **ROOMS:** 70 rooms
- **PRICE:** B&B €40-€120 per person. No single supplement. Look out for offers on website.

- **NOTES:** All major cards accepted. Restaurant serves dinner, 7pm-9pm, €50. Outdoor heated swimming pool and golf. Full wheelchair access. Pet friendly.

- **DIRECTIONS:**
The hotel is signposted from Kylemore. At Letterfrack, turn right, and travel 6.5km to hotel gates.
GPS 53.609167 -9.999167

SEA MIST HOUSE

Sheila Griffin
Clifden, Connemara
County Galway

☎ **+353 (0) 95-21441**
🖰 **www.seamisthouse.com**
📪 **sgriffin@eircom.net**

So, how do you define the essence of Bridgestone? What makes an address one of the 100 Best? Sheila Griffin defines the essence: she's one of the best.

A fine, handsome Victorian house, set just down the seaward road off the main square in Clifden, Sheila Griffin's Sea Mist B&B is one of those houses that defines the essence of Bridgestone.

It defines the essence of Bridgestone because what Ms Griffin does is personal, distinctive, artistic and creative. It's as if she treats Sea Mist house itself as an artist's palette, filling it with good cheer, good hospitality, a splendidly bohemian style and, most especially, with the wafting, aromatic allures of superb breakfast cooking early in the morning as the house and the guests come to life, as they look forward to scrambled eggs with honey-roasted salmon, or a fresh omelette with garden herbs, or American-style pancakes with crispy bacon and maple syrup, these being just a small assortment of the list of specialities guests are asked to choose from. The other attribute that singles Ms Griffin out is her ardent perfectionism, so Sea Mist is a house where everything is done as well as it can be.

● **OPEN:** Mar-Nov
● **ROOMS:** Four rooms, all en suite
● **PRICE:** €40-€60 per person sharing, single supplement €15-€25

● **NOTES:** Visa, Mastercard, Laser, Amex. No dinner. No wheelchair access. No facilities for children. Limited enclosed parking.

● **DIRECTIONS:**
Beside the Bank of Ireland in the town centre.
Sat Nav 53.4882 -10.0244.

SOUTH ARAN

Enda & Maria Conneely
Fisherman's Cottage
Inis Oirr, Aran Islands
📱 **+353 (0) 99-75073**
🖥 www.southaran.com
✉ foodwise@eircom.net

One of the great, left-field destinations of the Aran Islands, South Aran is an holistic experience, where food, place, attitude and calm reign.

You could go to Enda and Maria Conneely's quietly inspiring guesthouse and restaurant just to stay and eat, and to enjoy the charm of this singular island, and to revel in Enda's terrific cooking. That would be pretty perfect, to tell the truth.

Or you could do a powerboat course, or learn about macrobiotics, or do some pilates. And that would be pretty perfect, to tell the truth.

You could also do the 'Transformation Game', a life coaching course they teach. But, to tell you the absolute truth, you only need to come to the island and to stay and eat with these amazing people to undergo transformation in your life. Enda and Maria are holistic people, they are Zen, quietly spiritual, and genuinely inspiring in the most modest way. They put us in mind of the great aphorism from Shunryu Suzuki's book, *Zen Mind, Beginner's Mind*: "In the beginner's mind there are many possibilities; in the expert's mind there are few." South Aran offers many possibilities, all sublime.

● **OPEN:** Mar-Oct
● **ROOMS:** four rooms, all en suite.
● **PRICE:** B&B €40 per person sharing, €50 single occupancy

● **NOTES:** Visa, Access, Mastercard, Amex, Laser. Therapies and Consultations available. Adult only house. Breakfast and dinner in Fisherman's Cottage Restaurant.

● **DIRECTIONS:**
Take the ferry from Rossaveal or Doolin, or flight from Inverin. The House is a short walk from the pier. GPS 53.0673 -9.5314

CASTLEWOOD HOUSE

Helen & Brian Heaton
Dingle
County Kerry
📱 +353 (0) 66-915 2788
🖰 www.castlewooddingle.com
✉ castlewoodhouse@eircom.net

Castlewood House offers what is surely one of the finest breakfasts served anywhere in Ireland. But everything else here is just as spiffing.

Easter in Kerry, and time for all the McKennas to get a little south Kerry sea salt on their complexions, with a couple of days r'n'r in Helen and Brian Heaton's fine house in Dingle, in addition to cracking the bottle of bubbly to officially launch the Dingle Farmers' Market. "Fine" is just the right term for Castlewood, too: it's somewhat grand, and especially comfortable, with the rooms at the front enjoying views out across the water. Castlewood is the sort of place that Irish tourism needs in abundance. Brian and Helen run the house like the utter professionals they are, and they play to their strengths, in particular creating a breakfast offer that is one of the best in the country. But they also have time to chat, to impart information, to offer local knowledge, to make sure that you have what you need, even if you aren't entirely sure just what it is that you need. Style; comfort; service, yes, but above all there is an intimacy about staying in a house like Castlewood which means that you feel you are right at the centre.

● **OPEN:** Feb-Dec. Open over New Year.
● **ROOMS:** 12 rooms, all en suite.
● **PRICE:** B&B from €39-€75

● **NOTES:** Visa, Access, Mastercard, Laser. No dinner, but plenty of local restaurants within walking distance. Wheelchair access.

● **DIRECTIONS:**
From Dingle take R559 towards Slea Head river. House is just 5 minutes' walk from marina and acquarium.
GPS 52.141311 -10.286142

EMLAGH HOUSE

Marion & Grainne Kavanagh
Dingle
County Kerry
📞 **+353 (0) 66-915 2345**
🖱 **www.emlaghhouse.com**
✉ **info@emlaghhouse.com**

With new self-catering accommodation, complementing the
legendary stylishness of the
house, Emlagh has it all.

Emlagh is a grand and beautiful house, and to
complement their superb home, Marion and
Grainne have opened equally superb self-catering
accommodation, Water's Edge House, for those who
want to make a Dingle holiday into a major family stay-
over. The same breathtaking standards of housekeeping
and attention to detail that characterise Emlagh are
evident here: this is sumptuous accommodation, with
each apartment sleeping six people. Emlagh, meantime,
has been in our *Bridgestone 100 Best Places to Stay* book
ever since it opened, which says it all about this Dingle
landmark. Emlagh is distinguished by good taste, good
taste that is restrained, despite being understatedly
expensive, and by a pervasive luxury, and by the sort
of hospitality that offers you a cup of tea and some
superb home baking the very second that you walk
in the door. Grainne and Marion work hard, and have
that easy, confident, calm Kerry style of hospitality that
puts you at your ease from the second you arrive.

● **OPEN:** Mar-Oct
● **ROOMS:** 10 rooms
● **PRICE:** B&B €70-€110 per person sharing, €40
single supplement

● **NOTES:** Visa, Access, Mastercard, Amex, Laser. No
dinner. One room fully wheelchair accessible. Private car
park. No facilities for children under 8yrs.

● **DIRECTIONS:**
Upon arriving in Dingle, take the first exit from the
roundabout and Emlagh House is the first on left.
GPS 52.135119 --10.267133

TO GET AWAY FROM IT ALL

1
ANGLER'S RETURN
COUNTY GALWAY

2
BALLYVOLANE HOUSE
COUNTY CORK

3
BERVIE
COUNTY MAYO

4
CLIFF HOUSE HOTEL
COUNTY WATERFORD

5
DELPHI LODGE
COUNTY GALWAY

6
THE GLEN
COUNTY CORK

7
GORT NA NAIN FARM
COUNTY CORK

8
MONART
COUNTY WEXFORD

9
ROLF'S COUNTRY HOUSE
COUNTY CORK

10
ROUNDWOOD HOUSE
COUNTY LAOIS

HEATON'S HOUSE & RESTAURANT

Nuala & Cameron Heaton
The Wood, Dingle, County Kerry
📞 +353 (0) 66-915 2288
🖳 www.heatonsdingle.com
📧 heatons@iol.ie

With son David cheffing in the kitchen of their Shore View restaurant, Nuala and Cameron Heaton's guesthouse is upping the ante year after year.

Bridgestone editor Caroline Byrne put her finger on the pulse of Heaton's when she wrote that "Cameron and Nuala kept a constant presence should we ever have needed anything, and any request was instantly obliged". That presence explains why Heaton's succeeds so well as a place to stay, never mind the brilliant location and the amazing views out over Dingle harbour. But there is a powerful energy evident here, for their Shore View restaurant, with David Heaton in charge of the kitchen, has not only enjoyed great success in its first year, but has laid the grounds for plans to build a new restaurant later in the 2011 season. David's menus focus on local fish and shellfish, but there is also Kerry lamb and Hereford beef, and the cooking is classic, comforting and hip: seared scallops with Annascaul black pudding; Ventry crab claws in garlic butter; cod with creamed spinach and crispy pancetta; hake with courgette spaghetti. You could come to Heaton's in Dingle and find you never need to leave the house!

● **OPEN:** all year, except Dec-Feb. Open New Year.
● **ROOMS:** 16 rooms
● **PRICE:** €39-€65 per person, €46-€75 deluxe room, €55-€85 junior suite.

● **NOTES:**
Visa, Mastercard, Laser. Dinner available. Wheelchair access. Children welcome

● **DIRECTIONS:**
Overlooking the Harbour, just down from the Marina, near the roundabout in the centre of Dingle.
GPS 52.140594 -10.113581

HOTEL EUROPE

Michael Brennan
Fossa, Killarney
County Kerry
📱 **+353 (0) 64-667 1300**
🖥 **www.theeurope.com**
📧 **reservations@theeurope.com**

An utterly humongous hotel in terms of its sheer scale, but the team work hard, determined to make every guest feel very special indeed.

There are paradoxes in Michael Brennan's huge hotel, as Eamon Barrett points out: "A jaw-dropping investment has created a jaw-dropping spa at The Europe and the hotel, despite its size, tries its best to be intimate. A welcome at the steps, hot towels at the check in desk, stunning public areas, and views across the lakes that evoke Lake Como. Bedrooms might disappoint – until the next phase of upgrading is completed – and most guests seem to have realised that The Brasserie is the place to eat rather than the more formal Panorama Restaurant. The staff are excellent, the grounds are amazing and there is a sense that, whatever your request might be, The Europe will be able to fulfil it. What works against the hotel is its pure size, something which only become evident when you walk to the lake shore and turn around to look back at the leviathan you are staying in!" Solving the paradox of creating intimacy in such a large-scale setting is quite a feat, and it's still early days yet.

● **OPEN:** Mar-Oct
● **ROOMS:** 187 rooms and suites, all en-suite.
● **PRICE:** B&B from €110 per person sharing

● **NOTES:** All major cards accepted. Full disabled facilities. Espa Spa, swimming pool, tennis court, horse riding, fishing and many other activities available. Dining options include cafe, bar, lounge service and restaurant.

● **DIRECTIONS:**
Hotel is just outside city centre, take the N72, travelling in the direction of Killorglin you will see sign on left. GPS 52.067033 -9.571089

ISKEROON

Geraldine Burkitt & David Hare
Bunavalla, Caherdaniel
County Kerry
📱 **+353 (0) 66-947 5119**
🖱 **www.iskeroon.com**
📧 **res@iskeroon.com**

Nowhere else can match David and Geraldine's Iskeroon for that away-from-it-all feeling. So let's get lost.

Three bed-and-breakfast suites form the core of Iskeroon, but saying that is a bit like saying Rembrandt was a guy who painted pictures, including a few self-portraits and a few of his wife. What you need to know about David and Geraldine's Iskeroon is that its location is other-worldly wonderful: set in acres of semi-tropical gardens that run down to the sea, you feel you are in a world apart when you are here, and it's a feeling that stays with you always. The "other-worldly" aspect of this beautiful house, its other-worldly location at the water's edge, the sense of somehow being adrift from the mainland – though you are still on it, albeit only just – and the mix of design styles collated together in the suites, which fuse together so well, all conspire to create a luxe template of comfort in which to lose yourself. David and Geraldine have always been careful to safeguard "the personal touch and warm welcome people have come to expect at Iskeroon". It's right here.

● **OPEN:** 1 May-30 Sep
● **ROOMS:** Three suites. All can be self catering.
● **PRICE:** from €115 per suite. Single occupancy price on request.

● **NOTES:** Visa, Mastercard, Laser. Self-catering breakfast. No dinner. No wheelchairs. No facilities for children.

● **DIRECTIONS:**
From the Scarriff Inn between Waterville and Caherdaniel take sign to Bunavalla Pier. Go through gate marked 'private road', beside beach through pillars.
GPS 51.765278 -10.145278

THE KILLARNEY PARK HOTEL

Padraig & Janet Treacy
Kenmare Place, Killarney
County Kerry
📱 **+353 (0) 64-663 5555**
🖰 **www.killarneyparkhotel.ie**
📧 **info@killarneyparkhotel.ie**

The KP is one of the jewels of Irish hospitality, an hotel that is run the way all hotels should be. It's perfect in every way.

Padraig and Janet Treacy own two other hotels in Killarney, with the boutique The Ross and the grand The Malton, along with the Killarney Park. Each is different, and each will have its own admirers, but for us the all-round excellence of the KP just shades it. This hotel is, we think, one of the jewels of Irish hospitality. Why? Because every element of running an hotel, from housekeeping to cooking to the spa, is practised as an attempt at perfection. They don't just want to be the best they can be: they want to be The Best. And so, from the food in the bar to the style of the rooms, the KP is a masterpiece of the art of hospitality. But there is also something about the KP that feels – that is – enormously luxurious, right from the moment you walk in the door. There is a grandness to it, the conveying of a sense of well-being, that few other hotels can equal, and it is composed of sublime staff, sublime service, sublime comfort, sublime style. And that is why this is such a great destination.

- **OPEN:** All year, except Christmas
- **ROOMS:** 68 rooms
- **PRICE:** €250-€450 per room and suites

- **NOTES:** Visa, Mastercard, Amex, Laser. Restaurant & Bar, Dinner €65. Children welcome. Full disabled access. Swimming pool, spa.

- **DIRECTIONS:**
At 1st roundabout in Killarney (coming from Cork), take 1st exit for town centre. At 2nd roundabout take 2nd exit and at 3rd roundabout take 1st exit.
GPS 52.0647 -9.5142

THE PARK HOTEL

Francis & John Brennan
Kenmare
County Kerry
📱 **+353 (0) 64-664 1200**
🖱 **www.parkkenmare.com**
✉ **info@parkkenmare.com**

"Kick off your shoes and watch the world go by." That's the Eamon Barrett approach to staying in Kenmare's iconic Park Hotel. He's laid back!

It's like an old friend, the Park Hotel, someone whom you are always glad to see, someone with good taste, good stories to tell, lots of funny jokes. Here are Eamon Barrett's thoughts on its magic, from a staycation 2010 visit: "Higgledy-piggledy, cluttered, slightly faded, over furnished, The Park nonetheless is a wonderful place to stay", writes Eamon. "The staff treat it as if it's their own home, and it really is a place that makes you feel like kicking off your shoes and settling down to watch the world go by. Rooms are surprisingly spacious and quality is very high. No buffet here, everything is brought to your table. Service is extremely friendly and, more to the point, personal - on check-in, the person I had made the booking with came out to introduce herself. John Brennan is a constant presence and makes time to speak to everyone and seems genuinely interested in everyone." Mr Brennan and his superb team are the people who define this great hotel, with their grace and generosity.

● **OPEN:** Easter-Oct & 23 Dec-2 Jan.
● **ROOMS:** 46 rooms
● **PRICE:** B&B €196-€275 per person sharing. Suites & de luxe rooms €348-€423. Single €226-€275

● **NOTES:**
All major cards accepted. Restaurant open daily, Dinner from 7pm, €68. Wheelchair access. Secure parking. Luxury spa. 25m stainless-steel lap pool.

● **DIRECTIONS:**
At the top of Kenmare town.
GPS 51.877 -9.580

THE ROSS

Padraig & Janet Treacy
Town Centre, Killarney
County Kerry
📞 **+353 (0) 64-663 1855**
🖱 **www.theross.ie**
✉ **info@theross.ie**

The Ross was made over a couple of years back and transformed from a traditional hotel to a super-cool spot. The hospitality stayed the same.

Cool School meets Old School in The Ross. The Cool is the design, which is freakily wonderful and successful. The Old is the standard of service in the hotel, and the Cellar Restaurant and the Lane Café Bar, service that is rooted in traditional values of hospitality, discretion and charm. It's a wonderful mix of values, and one that very few manage to pull off successfully. The second of hotelier Padraig Treacy's trio of hotels in central Killarney, it is also the place where he was brought up and learnt his trade as a young man. Today, The Ross is a place where the correctness and the formality learnt during Mr Treacy's youth as he served his time in the business is practised as well as it ever was. Ireland is overrun with boutique hotels where comfort is sacrificed to style, and where the staff reckon attitude equals customer care. The Ross is different. So, The Cellar One dining room in the basement is tasteful and tasty, and the Lane Café Bar is a really cool spot for a drink or a bite to eat during the day. Truly, truly great.

- **OPEN:** All year, except Christmas
- **ROOMS:** 29 rooms and suites
- **PRICE:** B&B €160-€220 per room and suite

● **NOTES:**
All major credit cards accepted. Restaurant open for breakfast & dinner. Bar lunch. Wheelchair access. Private car parking. Leisure facilities of the Killarney Park Hotel.

● **DIRECTIONS:**
In the centre of Killarney, just round the corner from the main high street, beside the church.
GPS 52.05782 -9.50811

SHELBURNE LODGE

Tom & Maura Foley O'Connell
Killowen, Cork Road, Kenmare
County Kerry

📞 **+353 (0) 64-664 1013**
🖱 **www.shelburnelodge.com**
✉ **shelburnekenmare@eircom.net**

Maura and Tom's Shelburne Lodge is one of the most beloved of Irish destinations, a brilliant shining star.

If we ran things in Kenmare – and heaven knows it's not easy to run things in Kerry – there would be a statue erected to honour Maura Foley's service to the town, a level of service distinguished by stellar standards, the sort of standards she exhibits every day in her work with her husband, Tom, in Shelburne Lodge. Mrs Foley has gifted the Irish people with more than 45 years of masterly cooking and hospitality, and for us she is one of the true heroines of our food and hospitality cultures. But, Mrs Foley wouldn't like it if we did that, for she is self-effacing, modest, too busy to be interested in praise. Her house is one of the finest testaments to instinctive good taste that we know, which is why it is for many people their favourite Irish house. Everything is of a piece here: the design, the art, the cooking, the welcome, the gardens with their 200-year-old beech tree and 150-year-old pine tree. We don't know of another house where understatement in decor creates such a magical effect.

● **OPEN:** Mar-mid Dec
● **ROOMS:** Seven rooms, all en suite
● **PRICE:** €100-€170 per room. Single €80

● **NOTES:**
Visa, Mastercard, Laser.
No restaurant (good restaurants locally). Enclosed car parking. No wheelchair access. Low season special rates available. Children welcome, high chair, cot.

● **DIRECTIONS:**
300m from the centre of Kenmare, across from the golf course on the Cork road.

BALLYOGAN HOUSE

Robert & Fran Durie
Graiguenamanagh
County Kilkenny
☎ + 353 (0) 59-9725969
🖱 www.ballyoganhouse.com
✉ info@ballyoganhouse.com

Ballyogan is the kind of house that will have you smiling before you have walked in the door. When you are in, you'll find you'll smile even more.

It's such a pretty house, is Ballyogan, so secure in its place, so well sited, so well maintained. "The level of hospitality had me smiling all the way: beautiful house and lovely people", wrote Eamon Barrett of his encounter with this gem in the heart of one of Ireland's most beautiful areas, the Barrow Valley in and around Graiguenamanagh.

The Duries have that rare eye that can match the beauty of the surrounds with the beauty of the house itself. They have restored Ballyogan with perfect grace and suitability, directing everything towards a very welcoming comfort that makes you feel at home, just as some hot tea and cake, and superb breakfasts, will also make you feel right at home. It's not just the house that is in perfect order, mind you: the rolling lawns and mature trees seem as if they too have been arranged with benign care, and gazing out at them from the conservatory is a sublime, relaxing delight. Just the place from which to explore this beautiful, quiet region.

● **OPEN:** 1 Apr-31 Oct
● **ROOMS:** two twin rooms, one double and one family room
● **PRICE:** B&B €48-€50 per person sharing, single €58-€60

● **NOTES:** Visa, Mastercard, Laser. No wheelchair access. Dinner on request, €35-€40.

● **DIRECTIONS:**
From Graiguenamanagh take R705 New Ross rd for 4.5km. House is signposted on left from this road.
GPS 53.509444 -6.940083

THAT CHILDREN LOVE

1
**BALLYMALOE HOUSE
COUNTY CORK**

2
**BERVIE
COUNTY MAYO**

3
**CONNEMARA COAST HOTEL
COUNTY GALWAY**

4
**GREGAN'S CASTLE
COUNTY CLARE**

5
**KELLY'S RESORT HOTEL
COUNTY WEXFORD**

6
**LINSFORT CASTLE
COUNTY DONEGAL**

7
**LOUGH BISHOP HOUSE
COUNTY WESTMEATH**

8
**MORRISSEY'S
COUNTY CLARE**

9
**RENVYLE HOUSE
COUNTY GALWAY**

10
**RICHMOND HOUSE
COUNTY WATERFORD**

IVYLEIGH HOUSE

Dinah & Jerry Campion
Bank Place, Portlaoise
County Laois
📱 **+353 (0) 57-862 2081**
🖰 **www.ivyleigh.com**
✉ **info@ivyleigh.com**

Ivyleigh is the star of Portlaoise, thanks to Dinah Campion's meticulous and authoritative understanding of just exactly what hospitality is.

When we talk to people in the business about what customers want, we always stress "The Edit". What is "The Edit"? Well, it's what we do at Bridgestone, for instance. There are hundreds of places to stay in Ireland, but we reckon our readers only want the funkiest, most special, most alluring and best value places. So, we select 100 of them for you each year, leaving out hundreds of others, and that is this book. That is "The Edit". In a town house such as Ivyleigh, "The Edit" is what makes it a special place. "The Edit" is what signals Dinah Campion as a truly gifted practitioner, a person of taste and discrimination. There aren't forty things to eat at breakfast; there are simply those dishes Mrs Campion cooks to perfection, which are exactly what you want to eat. The house isn't lavish, grand, trendy or flummery: it is simply a beautiful townhouse, restored by an expert eye. And the comfort, then, comes from the apposite tableware, bath towels, toiletries, furnishings, all just right.

● **OPEN:** All year, except Christmas
● **ROOMS:** Six rooms, all en suite
● **PRICE:** B&B €40-€75 pps. Single room €55-€85

● **NOTES:** Visa, Mastercard. No dinner. No wheelchair access. On street car parking. Children over 8 years welcome.

● **DIRECTIONS:**
In Portlaoise, follow the sign for multi-storey car park. At car park entrance there is a sign with directions for Ivyleigh House.

ROUNDWOOD HOUSE

Hannah & Paddy Flynn
Mountrath
County Laois
☏ **+353 (0) 57-873 2120**
🖱 **www.roundwoodhouse.com**
✉ **info@roundwoodhouse.com**

One of those great country houses that seems to exist in its own universe and its own time, Hannah and Paddy's Roundwood House is just a peach.

'It's a treasure of a place", our friend Therese wrote about Roundwood, having partied with her family here for some 50th wedding celebrations. Therese is dead right. Roundwood is just the right house – a three-storey Palladian mansion – in just the right place – for us the Slieve Bloom region is one of the treasures of Ireland, and mercifully unspoilt and under-explored. Back in the 17th century, the estate was known as Friendstown, which seems to us to be just the perfect name. You come here with your friends. You make friends with the guests. And you will certainly make friends with Hannah and Paddy, who have taken over the running of this great destination from Hannah's folks, Frank and Rosemary Kennan. Frank and Rosemary made Roundwood into one of the glories of the Midlands over more than 25 years of service and hospitality, and Hannah and Paddy are going to keep on offering what Roundwood has always offered: timelessness and charm.

- ● **OPEN:** All year, except Christmas
- ● **ROOMS:** 10 rooms, all with private bathrooms
- ● **PRICE:** €60-€65 per person sharing. Single supplement €15

- ● **NOTES:** All major cards accepted. Dinner at 8pm, €35-€50, communal table. Book by noon. No wheelchair access. Recommended for children.

- ● **DIRECTIONS:**
Turn right at traffic lights in Mountrath for Ballyfin, then left onto R440. Travel for 5km on the R440.
GPS 53.024 -7.527

THE COURTHOUSE

Piero & Sandra Melis
Main Street, Kinlough
County Leitrim

📞 **+353 (0) 71-984 2391**
🖥 **www.thecourthouserest.com**
✉ **thecourthouserest@eircom.net**

Great Sardinian-influenced cooking, delicious Sardinian wines, and lovely simple rooms in pretty Kinlough: that's Piero's recipe for your stay.

If Piero Melis was cooking anywhere other than often-overlooked County Leitrim, his authentic, genuine Italian cooking would be celebrated and feted. But, in little Kinlough, close to the Donegal border, this quiet man and his lovely food gets little attention, save from the Bridgestone Guides and from local and visiting food lovers who know a good thing when they eat it, and who like the simplicity of the refurbished room, the simple comfort of the rooms upstairs, relishing the chance to do some surfing tomorrow on the good waves nearby. Mr Melis is from Sardinia, and he not only has the good wines of that lovely island, but also the quirks and culture of its cuisine. So, leave the bags and the surfboards upstairs, and get ready for linguini with sea urchin, spinach and ricotta ravioli, sirloin with rocket and rosemary, Thornhill duck with spinach and wild mushrooms, zuppa di mare, cooking with true soul, brother! Good service, good music, great wines, and a sweet and lovely outpost of goodness.

● **OPEN:** All year except Xmas. Thur-Sun only Oct-Feb
● **ROOMS:** Four rooms
● **PRICE:** B&B €37 per person sharing, €42 single

● **NOTES:** Visa, Mastercard, Laser. Wheelchair access. Restaurant opens for Dinner, 6.30pm-9.30pm, ('till 10pm high summer), and Sun lunch, noon-2.30pm. No wheelchair access to rooms.

● **DIRECTIONS:**
On the main street in Kinlough, on the bridge opposite the post office. GPS 54.450 -8.285

THE MUSTARD SEED

Daniel Mullane
Echo Lodge, Ballingarry
County Limerick
📞 **+353 (0) 69-68508**
🖰 **www.mustardseed.ie**
✉ **mustard@indigo.ie**

Dan Mullane's great country house and restaurant has been making people happy for more than 25 years.

Dan Mullane is a poet of the aesthetic world, a man whose grasp of design, comfort and style is matched by few others in Ireland. He is the kind of guy who can make a room seem like a stage set, so artfully and perfectly pitched is every design detail he conceives, in order to make a complete whole, a perfect unity. Both Echo Lodge, the country house, and its Mustard Seed restaurant, are blessed with the sort of classic charm that makes for a true icon of decor and comfort, a timeless summit of style that makes you swoon with delight. As with the design of the house, so it is with the cooking in The Mustard Seed restaurant, the sort of elegant country cooking that uses lots of modern methods – tempura; vegetable foams, confit – but which always serves forth food that is nothing other than Mustard Seed cooking, just the way we all love it, unpretentious country house cooking that never loses its focus on deliciousness. A few days in Echo Lodge in little Ballingarry is a balm for the soul, nothing less.

- **OPEN:** All year, except last 2 weeks in Jan & Xmas
- **ROOMS:** 18 rooms, including three suites
- **PRICE:** €65-€165 per person

- **NOTES:** Visa, Mastercard, Access. Dinner €62. Wheelchair access. Box room special rate €65 per person, sharing. Early bird menu options. Resident Thai masseuse.

- **DIRECTIONS:**
Take the Killarney road from Adare, 500m until you reach first turning off to the left, signed for Ballingarry. GPS 52.474672 -8.864692

NUMBER ONE PERY SQUARE

Patricia Coughlan
1 Pery Square, The Georgian Quarter
Limerick City, County Limerick
📱 **+353 (0) 61-402402**
🖰 **www.oneperysquare.com**
✉ **info@oneperysquare.com**

One Pery Square is not just the star of Limerick, but the very centre of Limerick hospitality and creative cooking.

Patricia Coughlan's No 1 Pery Square is the best thing to have happened to Limerick in years, and the hotel and restaurant have established themselves as the epicentre of Limerick's food culture. Ms Coughlan's boutique hotel has been one of the most completely conceived and delivered destinations in Ireland in recent years, and from the moment they opened their doors, the place was buzzing, not least because it is, quite simply, beautiful and comfortable. The rooms are beautiful, the cocktails are great, and Alan Burns' food is right in step, from pigeon with hazelnut purée and cherries to lamb's tongue and beetroot salad to turbot with baby artichokes These are big dishes and bold with flavour, and they deliver with the confidence that every aspect of Pery Square exudes. Ms Coughlan is a maverick, a person with a very clear vision, and a soul full of determination, and it all shows here in what is quite simply the star of Limerick city. Patricia Coughlan is a true food heroine, a hospitality maven.

- **OPEN:** All year, except 24-28 Dec
- **ROOMS:** 20 rooms, all en suite
- **PRICE:** €145-€195 per person sharing

- **NOTES:** All major credit cards accepted. Dinner available in Brasserie. Wheelchair access. Spa and wine shop. Valet car parking.

- **DIRECTIONS:**
On the corner of Pery Square and Barrington Street.

RIGNEY'S FARMHOUSE

Caroline & Joe Rigney
Curraghchase, Kilcornan
County Limerick
📞 **+353 (0) 61-393988**
🖰 **www.rigneysfarm.com**
📧 **info@rigneysfarm.com**

The bacon and sausages of the house are reared, made and cured by the woman of the house. Now, that is a sustainable Irish breakfast at its best.

It is always fascinating to see someone becoming a player. By "player" we mean someone whose work matters, who makes an original contribution in their field, who articulates a philosophy and who can express it in their work. We have known Caroline Rigney for several years now, and Mrs Rigney is becoming a player. In fact, Mrs Rigney is becoming a player on two fronts: as a superb B&B keeper in her farmhouse, and as a producer of some of the finest pork products you will find in Ireland. "Farmhouse" is perhaps a slightly misleading term, for this is actually a rather grand house, and there are lots of lovely rare-breed animals wandering around the fields, and there is a splendid farmshop from where Mrs Rigney retails her brilliant Curraghchase pork.

That pork, of course, is the mainstay of lovely breakfasts, and there is tea and home baking when you, the weary traveller, arrive here at Curraghchase. We will be hearing much more from Mrs Rigney, have no doubt about that, but right now she is doing just fine, thanks very much.

● **OPEN:** Open all year, except Christmas
● **ROOMS:** Four en suite rooms, including suites
● **PRICE:** €40-€50 per person sharing, €60 single

● **NOTES:** Working rare breed farm. Farm shop open Sun or by appt. No wheelchair access. 50% discount for children sharing room, children under 2 years free.

● **DIRECTIONS:**
In Kilcornan turn left into Curraghchase Forest Park and at the next crossroads turn right. They are the fourth house on left, clearly signposted.
GPS 52.603611 -8.191111

VIEWMOUNT HOUSE

Beryl & James Kearney
Dublin Road, Longford
County Longford
📱 **+353 (0) 43-334 1919**
🖥 **www.viewmounthouse.com**
✉ **info@viewmounthouse.com**

Fantastic cooking at breakfast and outstanding food in their hip restaurant makes Viewmount the brightest star in Longford's culinary history.

So, there are all the McKennas up in Longford, and up in Viewmount House as part of a little summer tour in the North West, and there we are in the restaurant, marvelling at the energy in the room – are they always this wild in Longford? – and marvelling at the quality of Gary O'Hanlon's cooking – the vegetarian degustation plate alone is worth the trip to Longford, it's such an artful, brilliantly conceived and superbly crafted starter. Viewmount is really two identities: the original house which dates from the 1740's where James and Beryl Kearney look after you, and the modern, hip restaurant where every Longford food lover – and many from much further afield – come to eat delicious, inventive cooking from Mr O'Hanlon which exploits the richness and variety that can be sourced from local artisans. All the McKennas ate superbly, both at dinner, and with a brilliant breakfast cooked by James that is served in one of the atmospheric rooms of the house, and which proved to be one of the highlight breakfasts of the year.

● **OPEN:** Open all year
● **ROOMS:** 12 rooms, all en suite
● **PRICE:** B&B €55-€65 per person

● **NOTES:** Visa, Mastercard, Laser, American Express. VM Restaurant open Wed-Sat 6.30pm-9.30pm & Sun lunch 1pm-4pm. €40-€55. Wheelchair access.

● **DIRECTIONS:**
From Longford town, take R393 to Ardagh. After 1km take right turn onto slip road and then follow signs to the house.
GPS 53.72246 -7.77105

GHAN HOUSE

Paul Carroll
Carlingford
County Louth
📱 **+353 (0) 42-937 3682**
🖱 **www.ghanhouse.com**
📧 **ghanhouse@eircom.net**

Paul Carroll is one of the unsung masterminds of modern Irish hospitality. Everything he and his team do in Ghan House is as good as it can be.

"Paul and his team were welcoming and generous. We loved it!" Isn't it amazing how some correspondents, with just a single sentence, can get straight to the heart of what makes a place special? Paul Carroll and his crew are welcoming. And they are generous. That welcoming nature, that generosity with time and effort, is why Ghan House is such an outstanding place to stay and eat. The narrative of Ghan House, the story of its hospitality, is based on making you feel welcome, and generously offering all the things you need. Without it, this would simply be a fine old house on the outskirts of a lovely village. But with it, Ghan is transformed, into something magical, welcoming, and generous. Human creativity. The cooking celebrates their location on Carlingford Lough and its fine fish and shellfish, and the availability of great lamb, beef and local mushrooms: crab ravioli with steamed samphire; gnocchi with wild mushrooms; Cooley lamb with blue cheese and tarragon soufflé. You will love it, my dears.

- **OPEN:** All year, except Christmas & New Year
- **ROOMS:** 12 bedrooms, all en suite
- **PRICE:** €105-€160 per person sharing, includes dinner

- **NOTES:** Visa, Mastercard, Access, Amex. Restaurant open six nights. No wheelchair access. Midweek and weekend breaks. Cookery school. Horse riding.

- **DIRECTIONS:**
First driveway on left after 50kph sign on entering Carlingford. 85km from Dublin, 69km from Belfast.
GPS 54.040278 -6.184167

BERVIE

John & Elizabeth Barrett
The Strand, Keel, Achill
County Mayo
📱 +353 (0) 98-43114
🖐 www.bervie-guesthouse-achill.com
📧 info@bervie-guesthouse-achill.com

For almost eighty years, John and Elizabeth's Bervie has been a happy home-from-home for visitors to Achill.

Something new

So, picture this: a day surfing or windsurfing on the Achill beaches, with great waves, toasty sunshine, bracing breezes, the hair and skin sand-flecked, the body exhausted at day's end. You head back to Bervie, and John opens a bottle of good wine as Elizabeth's cooking makes its way out of the kitchen to your table – smoked Achill salmon with pickled vegetables; roast rump of Achill lamb with pea purée, then some fruit crumble with ice cream. And tomorrow? The chance to do it all again! What a dream!

Except it isn't a dream. Bervie is here, waiting for you to get the wetsuit on and head down the garden and through the little wicket gate that opens onto the beach of Keel Strand, ready to conquer those waves. Guests have been coming here, to this old coastguard station, for almost 80 years, so hospitality is in the blood, hospitality is in the philosophy, and the philosophy is simple goodness, in food, in comfort, in peace, in contemplation of magnificent Achill Island.

- **OPEN:** Apr-Nov
- **ROOMS:** 14 rooms, all en-suite
- **PRICE:** B&B €50-€65 per person sharing. Weekly, full board rates also available.

- **NOTES:** Visa, Mastercard, Laser.
Dinner available in their restaurant. Wine list. Musical evenings, adjacent beach.

- **DIRECTIONS:**
In the village of Keel on Achill Island.
GPS 53.972686 -10.084319

ICE HOUSE

Claire O'Sullivan
The Quay, Ballina
County Mayo
📞 **+353 (0) 96-23500**
🖰 **www.theicehouse.ie**
✉ **chill@theicehouse.ie**

The Ice House is visually stunning, from the breathtaking location, to the rooms, to the food on the plate. It's the Vogue hotel of the north west.

Set hard by the banks of the River Moy, just several minutes' walk from Ballina town, the Ice House is visually stunning when you glimpse it first, which it needs to be to rival the views down-river at this idyllic location. Manager Dara Cruise has the good fortune to work with an excellent team – the crew in The Ice House are motivated, helpful, creative, courteous – and in the Pier Restaurant Gavin O'Rourke is producing elegant, original cooking, and, like everything else here, his cooking is particularly eye-fetching, with starters like tempura of monkfish with black ketchup and salsify dazzling you with its good looks before the tastes of the combination dazzle you one more time. Mr O'Rourke knows that we eat first with the eyes, and so halibut with saffron and a ragout of creamed leek with mussels and smoked salmon is perfect to look at and to eat, whilst a plum tarte tatin has pitch-perfect pastry. The rooms are gorgeous, modern and romantic, and everything in The Ice House is just perfectly chilled.

- ● **OPEN:** All year, except 25-26 Dec
- ● **ROOMS:** 32 bedrooms, all en suite
- ● **PRICE:** B&B €160-€190 per person

● **NOTES:**
Visa, Mastercard, Laser. Wheelchair access
Dinner served nightly from 6.30pm, lunch and bar menu also available.

● **DIRECTIONS:**
From Ballina follow road past Dunnes Stores. Take first exit on mini roundabout. Travel over bridge, take left turn onto N59. Take first left to Quay Road.

KNOCKRANNY HOUSE HOTEL

Adrian & Ger Noonan
Westport
County Mayo
📱 **+353 (0) 98-28600**
🖰 **www.khh.ie**
✉ **info@khh.ie**

Seamus Commons' food
has put this grand hotel
on the map, Knockranny
is firing on all cylinders.

Something new

"It's as if Seamus and Adrian are on a mission, hell-bent
to push the limits as far as they can go!" That's what
a local food-lover said to us about the ambitions of
chef Seamus Commons and Knockranny owner Adrian
Noonan, and their joint determination to make Knockranny into, well, the best hotel in the West, for starters and, bit by bit, one of the best hotels in Ireland,
full stop. It's a big ask, but there isn't a better or more
determined crew than the team at Knockranny. They
have already been winning the gongs and the prizes,
which is always good for confidence, but their confidence truly springs from a deep belief that they can
be the best, that they can be up there with The Park,
and Kelly's, and the Killarney Park and the other iconic
destinations. The hotel is grand and splendid, the spa is
excellent, and Mr Commons' cooking is simply some of
the best contemporary cooking happening in Ireland;
an alert, fascinating, meticulous and creative cuisine.
These guys are heading for the stars, simple as that.

- **OPEN:** All year
- **ROOMS:** 97 rooms, all en suite
- **PRICE:** B&B

- **NOTES:** Visa, Mastercard, Amex.
Restaurant open dinner, €54 Bar Lunch.
Full disabled facilities.

- **DIRECTIONS:**
Off the Dublin/Castlebar Road, 10mins from
Westport town centre.
GPS 53.80306 -9.50806

STELLA MARIS

Frances Kelly & Terence McSweeney
Ballycastle
County Mayo
☎ **+353 (0) 96-43322**
🖱 **www.StellaMarisIreland.com**
✉ **info@StellaMarisIreland.com**

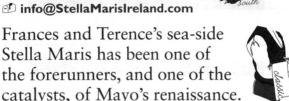

Frances and Terence's sea-side
Stella Maris has been one of
the forerunners, and one of the
catalysts, of Mayo's renaissance.

When we first wrote about Terence McSweeney and
Frances Kelly's country house, Stella Maris, way back in
2003, we predicted it would be one of the stars of the
decade. Everything a great country house needed was
in situ, not least the dynamism of this couple. For once,
we were right. Stella Maris is today recognised as one
of the best places to eat and stay in Ireland, and it has
gained that reputation thanks to the devotion and dis-
cipline of this couple, a pair of fastidious hotel keepers.
Ms Kelly's cooking, in particular, is amazing: modestly
and precisely executed in every detail. It is food that
comforts and delights, and it reminds us in many ways
of the cooking of Ballymaloe House, country cooking
ennobled by classy ingredients, cooking that has the
most complete confidence of all: the confidence to be
simple, the confidence to let the food be itself, and to
taste of itself, whether you are having Ballycastle lamb,
or scallops with polenta, or a perfect poached peach.
Delightful.

- ● **OPEN:** Easter-early Oct
- ● **ROOMS:** 11 rooms
- ● **PRICE:** B&B €200-€260 per room

● **NOTES:** Visa, Mastercard. Wheelchair access. Limited
ability to accommodate young children. A la carte dinner
served 7pm-9pm.

● **DIRECTIONS:**
Go down the hill from Ballycastle, and the Stella Maris
is signposted from here. Turn right, it's on the Pier Road,
overlooking the sea.
GPS 54.298484 -9.388575

FOR WEDDINGS

1
**ABERDEEN LODGE
COUNTY DUBLIN**

2
**BALLYMALOE HOUSE
COUNTY CORK**

3
**BALLYNAHINCH CASTLE
COUNTY GALWAY**

4
**GHAN HOUSE
COUNTY LOUTH**

5
**GOUGANE BARRA HOTEL
COUNTY CORK**

6
**KELLYS RESORT HOTEL
COUNTY WEXFORD**

7
**MACNEAN TOWNHOUSE
COUNTY CAVAN**

8
**THE MUSTARD SEED
COUNTY LIMERICK**

9
**NUMBER ONE PERY SQUARE
COUNTY LIMERICK**

10
**OLDE POST INN
COUNTY CAVAN**

WESTPORT PLAZA

John Clesham
Castlebar Street, Westport
County Mayo
📱 **+353 (0) 98-51166**
🖱 **www.westportplazahotel.ie**
📧 **info@westportplazahotel.ie**

The superb team in the Plaza are simply masters of the art of hospitality. Stay in Westport for a couple of days, and they'll show you how it's done.

Excellent staff are the USP of the Westport Plaza, and when we say excellent, and when we say Unique Selling Point, we mean both, and we mean both of these at their highest level: these guys are the bee's knees of hospitality and they transform a night in the hotel, or dinner in the restaurant, into a little treasure of good feelings. Their achievement is considerable, for what they do is to inject that vital human magic into every element of the hotel. Ireland has lots of luxury hotels that are not luxurious at all, simply because there is no true service, no genuine customer care, no real Irish hospitality. But the very things that make Irish hospitality so good, so inimitable, are to be found here – a human animus, a human concern, a human generosity that will go the extra mile in order to make sure that you have what you need, and an intelligence that knows that what you need, in an hotel above all else, is someone to watch over you. The Plaza crew do just that, so stay for a few days and get all the benefits of a masterclass in the art of service.

● **OPEN:** All year including Christmas
● **ROOMS:** 87 rooms, all en suite
● **PRICE:** B&B €49-€160 per person sharing

● **NOTES:** Visa, Mastercard, Laser, Amex. Wheelchair access. Full restaurant facilities

● **DIRECTIONS:**
As you approach the town from Castlebar, the hotel is at the first set of traffic lights on your right-hand side. GPS 53.801261 -9.518608

BELLINTER HOUSE

Cora Dwyer
Navan
County Meath
📱 **+353 (0) 46-9030900**
🖱 **www.bellinterhouse.com**
📧 **info@bellinterhouse.com**

Bellinter may be almost too-cool-for-school, but a rigorous professionalism underlies the actions of the staff and the kitchen crew in this ace place.

Jay Bourke and John Reynold's Bellinter has had its ups and downs as the recession rumbles on in Ireland. It's a project that we need to see survive, for Bellinter has been one of the most beautifully realised hotel projects in Ireland in recent times. Quite simply, this is one of the most sublime places to stay in Ireland, a design icon where the history of the house has been beautifully assimilated and acknowledged in the context of the needs and demands of the modern age.

Bellinter is different: the house lives for the modern era thanks to the subtle use of technology, and thanks to fantastic service, an amazing pool, and good food in the Eden restaurant. This is a house that knows and understands exactly what luxury actually is: cocoon-like rooms that are just the right size; superbly confident service that is understated in manner but utterly efficient and professional; and the Bellinter pool gets our vote as the best pool in the country. Hip, knowing, and lovely, and one of the great getaways from Dublin.

● **OPEN:** All year
● **ROOMS:** 34 rooms
● **PRICE:** B&B midweek from €69, weekends from €89 per person sharing

● **NOTES:** Eden Restaurant serves breakfast, 8am-11am and dinner, 6pm-9pm. Food served in Drawing Room and Bellinter Bar 11am-10pm. Swimming pool, and library.

● **DIRECTIONS:**
From the N3, turn at the Tara na Ri pub, drive 3km and Bellinter House is on your right-hand side.

COOPERSHILL HOUSE

Simon O'Hara
Riverstown
County Sligo
☏ **+353 (0) 71-916 5108**
🖱 **www.coopershill.com**
✉ **reservations@coopershill.com**

Something new

A new generation of the O'Hara family brings energy and passion to one of the great Irish country houses.

"We are proud of what we do and would love to share it!", Simon O'Hara wrote to us, and when people write about their pride in their work, it rings our bell, so off we all went to Sligo. Coopershill has always been one of the most beautiful and beautifully maintained of the classic Irish country houses, and Simon and Christine McCauley have brought a new burnish of energy to the patina of age that graces Coopershill. It's a fabulously comfortable place, where time stops when you have afternoon tea, but where the tempo of energy and conversation picks up in the dining room as Ms McCauley's food makes its way out – garden spinach soup; smoked estate venison in a salad; rack of lamb; Donegal hake; a sublime cauliflower gratin that touches the perfection which is reached by a gooseberry tart served with gooseberry and elderflower ice cream, a pudding that was one of the great dishes of 2010. Breakfast next morning was superb, and the McKennas all had a great time at Coopershill. Oh, that pudding!

● **OPEN:** Apr-Oct
● **ROOMS:** Eight rooms, all en suite
● **PRICE:** B&B €99-€122 per person sharing

● **NOTES:** Visa, Mastercard, Laser. Children welcome tennis court, gardens, croquet. walks. Pets can overnight in owner's car. No disabled facilities. Afternoon tea €5, for residents, Picnics €13 pp, light lunch €15

● **DIRECTIONS:**
On N4, 19km south east of Sligo. At Drumfin crossroads follow signs.
GPS 54.1381 -8.4154

INCH HOUSE

Mairin Byrne
Thurles
County Tipperary
📞 **+353 (0) 504-51261/51348**
🖥 **www.inchhouse.ie**
✉ **mairin@inchhouse.ie**

The Egan family's range of artisan foods is the perfect complement to their beautiful country house. Is there anything that these guys can't do?!

There is an energy in Inch House, as the dynamic Egan family, headed by John and Nora's daughter, Mairin, have evolved from the core business of their splendid country house and restaurant, and begun to make and market a terrific range of specialist foods, including a truly fab black pudding which is made for them by the brilliant TJ Crowe of Dundrum. In addition to the pudding, there are fine fruit sauces and true-tasting relishes – mango chutney, plum chutney, red onion marmalade and red pepper relish. This is a logical, smart move, for Inch is one of the standard bearers in Tipperary for hospitality and dedication to cooking and service that is selfless and devoted. So, come and stay for the night in comfort, eat Michael Galvin's delicious country cooking in their grand and graceful restaurant and, after a wonderful breakfast the next morning, fill up a basket with good things and take the taste of Inch House home with you to savour the experience a little longer. You'll be so glad you did.

● **OPEN:** All year, except Christmas & Easter
● **ROOMS:** Five rooms, all en suite
● **PRICE:** €50-€60 per person sharing, Single supplement €10

● **NOTES:**
Visa, Master, Laser, Dinner 6.30pm-9.30pm Tue-Sat. No wheelchair access.

● **DIRECTIONS:**
6.4km from Thurles on the Nenagh Road, R498. Turn off at the Thurles exit on the main M8 road.
GPS 52.7211183 -7.92173333

THE OLD CONVENT

Dermot & Christine Gannon
Clogheen
County Tipperary
📞 **+353 (0) 52-746 5565**
🖳 **www.theoldconvent.ie**
✉️ **info@theoldconvent.ie**

Not just a getaway, but a hide-away. And not just a hideaway, but a gourmet hideaway. Meet The Old Convent in Clogheen.

We like the way Dermot and Christine Gannon do things. Other chefs and country house keepers would likely strive to create a "Gourmet Getaway". But Christine and Dermot created a "Gourmet Hideaway" when they opened The Old Convent. It's a small distinction, but an important one. They have fashioned a design style that is both big and bold, and yet minimalistically understated – big white walls undershot with dashes of deep colour. It feels, therefore, like a place to hide away, to find personal space, private time.

The cooking is beyond good, and is one of the glories of modern Irish gastronomy. As Eamon Barrett writes: "Breakfast puts the tin hat on what has been, truly, a near-perfect experience: organic yoghurt with fresh fruit and caramelised pecans. A flute of Traas' organic sparkling apple juice; magnificent organic scrambled eggs with mushrooms. Brown bread and amazing fruit bread. And finally, a lovely goodbye. Is it any surprise that all of the rooms were full?" No surprise, Eamon.

● **OPEN:** All year, except Christmas-end Jan. Weekends only off season.
● **ROOMS:** Seven rooms, all en suite
● **PRICE:** B&B €80-€95 per person sharing, €40 single supplement

● **NOTES:**
Visa, Mastercard, Laser. Dinner in restaurant Thu-Sat, one seating, 8-course tasting menu, €65. No wheelchair access. Private car parking. Not suitable for children.

● **DIRECTIONS:**
On the R668 Cahir to Lismore road.

CLIFF HOUSE HOTEL

Adriaan Bartels
Ardmore
County Waterford
📞 **+353 (0) 24-87800**
🖱 **www.thecliffhousehotel.com**
📧 **info@thecliffhousehotel.com**

The Cliff House is worth every word of the capacious praise it has earned since they opened the doors of this jewel.

Staying at the Cliff House, you can sometimes feel that you have fallen off the edge of the world, and tumbled into some magical dream-state/ dream-scape. Hey, it happened to Alice, so why not you! So, in this new dream place, every room looks out over the sea, and the design is elementally beautiful, the colour palette is lurid and slightly camp, the food is provocative and smart, the service is polite, everyone is having a good time, and the workaday world seems a million, trillion miles away.

That's precisely the illusion a great hotel should create, and the fact that they do it so well in the Cliff House is testament to the skills of manager Adriaan Bartels and chef Martijn Kajuiter. Their hard work has met with great success, so much so that they have opened the Cliff House Townhouse in Dublin, though that address needs more time to match the polish and confidence of the Ardmore hotshot. So, tumble into a dream in lovely Ardmore: it can prove to be an unforgettable experience.

- **OPEN:** all year except Christmas
- **ROOMS:** 39 rooms
- **PRICE:** B&B from €180 per room

- **NOTES:** All major cards accepted. Wheelchair access. Restaurant open for dinner, €65-€85. Bar serves food noon-9pm. Loc8 code YSB-80-TR9

- **DIRECTIONS:**
From the N25 turn onto the R673 signposted Ardmore. Once in Ardmore take the Middle Road to the hotel.
GPS 51.948614 -7.715078

GLASHA FARMHOUSE

Olive O'Gorman
Ballymacarbry
County Waterford
📱 **+353 (0) 52-613 6108**
🖰 **www.glashafarmhouse.com**
🖃 **glasha@eircom.net**

What do you do in Olive O'Gorman's famous Glasha Farmhouse? Walking, eating, drinking, enjoying yourself. What more could anyone need?

When PJ McKenna and his Dad made their last trip to Olive O'Gorman's celebrated country house, they contented themselves with some relatively short local walks into and around the village and back, along with the walk down to the pub at the bridge for a pint of stout and a glass of pop.

But as PJ gets a wee bit older, the pair are hatching plans for more extensive walks when they get back to Olive's house: serious hikes in the Ballymacarbry hills, in the Waterford ranges, all day adventures on foot, exploring this most blessed part of the country. And what will sustain the pair of them will be two things: the brilliant breakfast they will have enjoyed in Olive's charming dining room, and the promise of a true farmhouse dinner to restore body and soul when they get back, sodden, foot-sore and weary. Sure, who cares about that, for Olive's country cooking is amongst the best restoratives we know, and after the sleep of the just, they'll lace up the boots, and go again.

● **OPEN:** Jan-Dec
● **ROOMS:** Six rooms, all en suite
● **PRICE:** B&B €50-€60 per person sharing. Single supplement €60-€70

● **NOTES:** Visa, Mastercard, Laser. Dinner 8.30pm €45. Children over 12 years welcome. Secure parking. Wheelchair access.

● **DIRECTIONS:**
Well signposted, off the R671 between Clonmel and Dungarvan. 3km from Ballymacarbry.
GPS 52.276058 -7.759528

PASTIS @ GLENCAIRN INN

Fiona & Stéphane Tricot
Glencairn, Lismore
County Waterford

📞 **+ 353 (0) 58-56232**
🖰 **www.glencairninn.com**
📧 **info@glencairninn.com**

A beautiful example of an old coaching inn where simple luxury is married to simple and delicious cooking and the welcome of Fiona and Stéphane.

"Brilliant to stay overnight. Great food!"
Well, that is the sort of encomium we are always happy to receive from friends who have been touring the country with their *Bridgestone Guides*, enjoying the collection of idiosyncratic and – let's be honest – sometimes even eccentric, hoteliers and country house keepers and B&B masters whom we collate and select for this book each year. Since taking over the beautiful Glencairn Inn, a flower-decked old coaching inn of low ceilings, a bar, intimate rooms and a cosy dining room that looks like it has sprung fresh-born from the pages of *Country Living*, Stéphane and Fiona have been doing the good thing, cooking nice French-inflected food in the bistro, maintaining the character of the house thanks to expert hospitality, establishing yet another exceptional destination address in beautiful West Waterford. The Glencairn Inn has much of the dream archetype about it, which explains why our friends reported so vividly on their stay here, and enjoyed it so much. Quite lovely.

● **OPEN:** All year, except three weeks in Jan
● **ROOMS:** Five rooms
● **PRICE:** €85 per room, €55-€60 for single room

● **NOTES:**
Visa, Mastercard, Laser. Dinner in Pastis Bistro, €40
Seasonal offers available for dinner + B&B.
No wheelchair access. Petanque court.

● **DIRECTIONS:**
3km from Lismore and signposted from the N72.

RICHMOND HOUSE

Paul & Claire Deevy
Cappoquin
County Waterford
📞 +353 (0) 58-54278
🖰 www.richmondhouse.net
✉ info@richmondhouse.net

Paul and Claire Deevy are
master and mistress of one
of the great Waterford
treasures, the fab Richmond.

Paul and Claire Deevy, who cook in and run the delightful Richmond House, aren't really professional people,
we don't think. Yes they are trained and they've been to
the schools and colleges and whathaveyou. But, first and
foremost, we think that they are people people, with
professionalism built into the equation in order to make
sure everything runs smoothly in their country house
hotel. But, from the off, their instinct is to look after
and to mind the customer as another human being, as a
guest, a friend, rather than as a customer.

Mr Deevy cooks with quiet confidence and flair, never
showing off, his dedication always at the service of
his superb ingredients. He taught us one of our most
profound lessons about food many years ago, when he
explained that the superb lamb we had enjoyed "would
have grazed on pastures that had never been ploughed".
So, lamb is always a great dinner choice, but so are the
Helvick scallops, the McGrath's sirloin; the Skeghanore
duck with sage and onion stuffing. Sweet, lovely place.

● **OPEN:** All year except Christmas
● **ROOMS:** Nine rooms
● **PRICE:** from €60 per person sharing, Single
supplement €20

● **NOTES:**
All major cards accepted. Restaurant open for dinner
only, Mon-Sun (closed on Sun in winter), €28-€55
Private parking. Children welcome, babysitting, toys.

● **DIRECTIONS:**
Just outside Cappoquin, the house is well signposted.
GPS 52.139261 -7.846708

THE TANNERY TOWNHOUSE

Paul & Máire Flynn
10 Quay Street, Dungarvan
County Waterford
☎ **+353 (0) 58-45420**
🖱 **www.tannery.ie**
✉ **info@tannery.ie**

Two townhouses, a cookery school, a kitchen garden, and a brilliant restaurant. Paul and Maire take it all in their stride.

All of the McKennas decamped to Dungarvan earlier in the year to enjoy the town's annual food festival, and let us tell you that this is one of the best-organised food festivals in the county, with an atmosphere in the town at the Sunday morning market that is only electric. To find yourself staying in The Tannery Townhouse, eating dinner in The Tannery Restaurant, and then enjoying the buzz of the town itself is a truly mighty experience – local people; local foods; local beers (we love 'em!); local culture, it was a blast. And, of course, we reckon that without people like Paul and Maire Flynn, such a festival would never have happened. When we wrote about The Tannery back in the mid 1990's, this region, never mind this town, had no culinary reputation whatsoever. The Flynns and others have built their food culture from scratch, and to celebrate it with them is a mighty privilege, especially when you do so from the stylish comfort of these two beautiful Tannery Townhouses.

● **OPEN:** All year, except late January
● **ROOMS:** 14 rooms, all en suite
● **PRICE:** from €50 per person sharing, Single €70

● **NOTES:** Visa, Mastercard, Laser, Amex. Tannery Restaurant is open for dinner Tue-Sat, 6pm-9.30pm. Lunch Fri & Sun. Cookery School.

● **DIRECTIONS:**
20m from The Tannery Restaurant, beside the Old Market House building.
GPS 52.08864 -7.61677

LOUGH BISHOP HOUSE

Helen & Christopher Kelly
Derrynagarra, Colinstown
County Westmeath
📱 **+ 353 (0) 44-9661313**
🖥 **www.loughbishophouse.com**
📧 **chkelly@eircom.net**

Lough Bishop House is the
most gorgeous, vital, farmhouse and farm, and Chris and
Helen are inspiring farmers.

If we wanted to show you the culture of agriculture
at work, in all its philosophical, contemplative and
active glory, then we would suggest you spend a few
days with Christopher and Helen at Lough Bishop
House. Even just a few days here will show you a mixed
organic farm where everything – everything! – enjoys
optimum health, where everything shines with vigour
and nature, from animals to field mushrooms, from
horses to the orchard. In fact, were we in the posi-
tion to do it, we would love to make a television series
about Lough Bishop, as it ravels through the seasons of
a year. We would call it "Helen and Christopher's agri-
CULTURE", and it would open people's minds to what
farming is meant to be about, because it would show
farming in step with nature, in step with place, in step
with all the exciting, elemental things that tie us to the
earth. Lough Bishop is important, and you should stay
here to be reminded of the things that make us human.
Oh, and the hosts are ace and the food is simply fab.

● **OPEN:** All year, except Christmas and New Year
● **ROOMS:** Three rooms, including family room
● **PRICE:** B&B €55 per person sharing, €10 single
supplement

● **NOTES:** No credit cards. Dinner, book before noon,
7pm, €30. Working farm. No wheelchair access.

● **DIRECTIONS:**
From Castlepollard take the R394 Mullingar road, turn
left opposite Whitehall School and Church, L5738.
2km up that road on the right-hand side.
GPS 53.6344166 -7.26471666

TEMPLE

Declan & Bernadette Fagan
Horseleap, Moate
County Westmeath
📞 **+353 (0) 57-933 5118**
🖰 **www.templespa.ie**
✉ **relax@templespa.ie**

A true spa is a place of holistic healthfulness, a place that
heals the soul as well as the
body: that's what Temple is.

Declan and Bernadette Fagan's Temple could
not be better named. What is a temple? "Edi-
fice dedicated to accommodation or service of god(s)",
says our old Concise Oxford Dictionary, and in this
most singular retreat and spa, run by this amazing
couple, the god being accommodated and enjoying the
fantastic service is: you. Relax: you're worth it. You
know you are. Temple is a true spa, by which we mean
that it is motivated by an holistic, healthful vision of life.
It's not just a place for the wives of the bourgeoisie to
spend money. Instead it is a place dedicated to well-
ness. The comfort is here to make you feel well, the
spa is here to make you feel well, the delicious, healthy
cookery is here to make you feel well. At the centre
of all this are Declan and Bernadette Fagan, and at the
centre of their work is their vision of health. They are
a most singular couple, blessed with great gifts, great
generosity, and they are that rarity these days: they are
wise people. A temple for body, and soul.

● **OPEN:** All year, except Christmas
● **ROOMS:** 23 rooms, all en suite
● **PRICE:** All inclusive rates: two nights B&B plus one
dinner, €199, includes use of the spa facilities and the
option to participate in the daily activity programme.

● **NOTES:** Visa, Mastercard, Access, Amex. Restaurant
open for Dinner, 7pm-9pm. Wheelchair access. Children
over 15 years only. Inclusive rates, see website.

● **DIRECTIONS:**
1km off the N6 Dublin-Galway road, clearly signposted.
GPS 53.4052 -7.6036

ON THE BEACH

1
BERVIE
COUNTY MAYO

2
CLIFF HOUSE HOTEL
COUNTY WATERFORD

3
DOLPHIN BEACH
COUNTY GALWAY

4
ISKEROON
COUNTY KERRY

5
KELLY'S RESORT HOTEL
COUNTY WEXFORD

6
KILMURVEY HOUSE
COUNTY GALWAY

7
LINSFORT CASTLE
COUNTY DONEGAL

8
RATHMULLAN HOUSE
COUNTY DONEGAL

9
ROCK COTTAGE
COUNTY CORK

10
STELLA MARIS
COUNTY MAYO

WINEPORT LODGE

Jane English & Ray Byrne
Glassan, Athlone
County Westmeath
☎ **+353 (0) 90-643 9010**
🖥 **www.wineport.ie**
✉ **lodge@wineport.ie**

Every element syncs with every other element in the artful Wineport, one of Ireland's greatest getaways.

Cathal Moran, the chef at Wineport Lodge is one of those talents who we think is going to become a major player over the next few years. There is flair and technique to his food, but also an appreciation of ruddiness – he has a countryman's love of good food, a respect for the work of artisans and speciality producers, which means his sourcing is as careful as his cooking, and he likes the elemental flavours of game birds, of blue cheese, the sweetness of seared scallops, and he likes to frame his ingredients within the classic template of European styles, with the occasional diversion off to the Far East. His cooking works wonderfully well within the surroundings of Ray Byrne and Jane English's lakeside boutique hotel, a destination which is one of the great escapes in Ireland, a place where time stops from the second you arrive in the car park and catch that first glimpse of the glinting water of Lough Ree. The service, the comfort, the design are all of a piece, fashioned with a watchmaker's precision, just perfect.

- **OPEN:** All year
- **ROOMS:** 29 rooms
- **PRICE:** B&B from €79 per person sharing. Upgrades and weekend breaks also available.

- **NOTES:** All major cards accepted. Restaurant serves dinner, à la carte menu approx €65. Wheelchair access.

- **DIRECTIONS:**
At Athlone, take the Longford exit off Dublin/Galway rd, fork left at the Dog & Duck. Lodge is 1.5km further on on the left.
GPS 53.465578 -7.883470

KELLY'S RESORT HOTEL

Bill Kelly
Rosslare
County Wexford
📱 **+353 (0) 53-913 2114**
🖐 **www.kellys.ie**
📭 **info@kellys.ie**

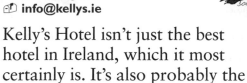

Kelly's Hotel isn't just the best hotel in Ireland, which it most certainly is. It's also probably the most successful hotel in Ireland.

In a year when Irish hotel occupancy rates hovered around the disastrously precarious figure of 50% – and we think that's an optimistic figure – Bill Kelly's hotel had an occupancy rate in excess of 90%, and made a profit. That's no surprise. Kelly's is not like other hotels, and it isn't run like other hotels. Bill Kelly and his extraordinary team, for instance, didn't retrench during the severe economic climate. Instead, they focused on improving service, the only way to convert the first-time customer into a regular customer. It is in ways like this that Kelly's is unique: the focus on making sure the customer is having a wonderful time at each and every moment of their stay at this glorious hotel is all that the Kelly's team care about. Add in glam comfort, a fantastic art collection – do buy their lovely book, *For the Love of Art*: it's a peach of a publication – superlative cooking that is amongst the best in the country, and there you have Kelly's Hotel, the envy of every other hotel in Ireland.

- ● **OPEN:** Late Feb-early Dec
- ● **ROOMS:** 120 rooms, all en suite
- ● **PRICE:** Spring/autumn: weekend €299pp; 5-day midweek from €550pp; Summer: 7-day rate from €975pp. Shorter breaks available. All full board.

- ● **NOTES:** All major cards accepted. All rates include full board. La Marine restaurant also comes recommended. Wheelchair access. Every facility for children & babies.

- ● **DIRECTIONS:**
Clearly signposted in Rosslare.

McMENAMIN'S

Seamus & Kay McMenamin
6 Glena Terrace
Spawell Road, Wexford

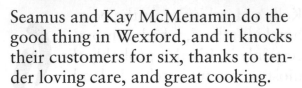

📱 **+ 353 (0) 53-914 6442**
🖐 **www.wexford-bedandbreakfast.co**
📁 **info@wexford-bedandbreakfast.com**

Seamus and Kay McMenamin do the good thing in Wexford, and it knocks their customers for six, thanks to tender loving care, and great cooking.

Everyone's reaction to staying at Seamus and Kay's Wexford B&B is utterly predictable. Stay here for a day or two, and you fast become converts to the cult of McMenamin's. And, as converts, you are charged with spreading the good news on behalf of McMenamin's. As proselytisers, they spread the gospel of the hospitality of this couple, and they spread it with the zeal of fundamentalists, of people who have seen the light, glimpsed the truth, have been vouchsafed the one true way. We get so many letters from delighted guests who have stayed at Glena Terrace and who have, in particular, been wowed! by Kay's breakfasts, that we could paper all the walls of the B&B with them. What a wonderful testimony to the power of hospitality that the receiver simply has to pass on the message, has to win new converts to the cause, has to write to the critics to let them know how special McMenamin's is. Well, we know that very well ourselves: we know how singular this couple are, how they make their magic.

● **OPEN:** Mar-Dec
● **ROOMS:** Four rooms
● **PRICE:** B&B from €45-€50 per person sharing

● **NOTES:**
Visa, Mastercard, Laser.
No dinner.
Wheelchair access.

● **DIRECTIONS:**
In the centre of Wexford, opposite the County Hall.

MONART

Mark Browne
The Still, Enniscorthy
County Wexford
☎ **+353 (0) 53-923 8999**
🖰 **www.monart.ie**
📧 **reservations@monart.ie**

"A visit to Monart is a true luxury treat", says Eamon Barrett. Beautiful house, brilliant staff. Here's his report.

"On check-in we were greeted with 'Welcome back'. We were reminded that on our last visit we had a room facing the lake, and that this time we would be facing the gardens. The room was immaculate and did indeed open out onto the grounds via a huge sliding door. Later, some drinks served lakeside were delivered by staff who all seemed to have just received wonderful news, such was their united state of good humour. The property is immensely impressive and maturing beautifully - there isn't so much as a blade of grass out of place. The noise of the ducks on the lake, the cascade of water from the man-made waterfall and the reassuring presence of a team of professional staff make for a truly serene experience. Does Monart have a weak spot? Well, the food at dinner does not live up to the standard set by the rest of the experience but this is nitpicking of the highest order. Liam Griffin's achievement in creating Monart and his commitment to its maintenance is to be applauded." He'll be back.

● **OPEN:** All year, except Christmas
● **ROOMS:** 70 rooms
● **PRICE:** €95-€250 per person sharing, €695 upwards for suite, depending on dates and availability, single supplement €40

● **NOTES:** Visa, Master, Amex. Dinner, €39.50. Wheelchair access. Over 18 yrs only. Spa open 9am-9pm. No functions. D+ B&B rates quoted, see website.

● **DIRECTIONS:**
Just off the N11 road to Gorey. See map on website.
GPS 52.513889 -6.613889

BALLYKNOCKEN HOUSE

Catherine Fulvio
Glenealy, Ashford
County Wicklow
📱 **+353 (0) 404-44627**
🖱 **www.ballyknocken.com**
📧 **info@ballyknocken.com**

"A challenging year, but sure that brings out the best in us!" says Catherine Fulvio. This girl should be our new President!

Having made her television debut last year, Catherine Fulvio has returned with great success to the small screen, and along the way she has become a cover girl, debuting on the pages of *Food & Wine* magazine. She's up in the stratosphere now, but her feet are firmly rooted in Ballyknocken, her mother's house, and her house, her school, her B&B, her centre of the universe. It's typical of the way in which she works that Mrs Fulvio's telly series aren't smash-bang global hits. Instead, they are cult shows: those who love them, love them big time, just as those who love Ballyknocken love it big time, and those who love Mrs Fulvio's cookery classes love them big time. That's the sort of idiosyncratic and very personal approach that Mrs Fulvio has as a cook, as a teacher, and as an hostess: she isn't mainstream, for there is too much going on in her voracious brain for her to ever bow to the mainstream. Ballyknocken is a wonderful house, run by an exceptional woman, a true cult success story.

● **OPEN:** mid Jan-mid Dec
● **ROOMS:** Seven rooms
● **PRICE:** From €50-€69 per person sharing.

● **NOTES:** Visa, Mastercard. Dinner, Fri, Sat €45. No wheelchair access. Cookery school.

● **DIRECTIONS:**
From Dublin, head south to Ashford (on N11), then turn right after Chester Beatty pub. Continue for 5km and the house is on the right.
GPS 52.9769666 -6.14308333

THE BROOK LODGE INN

Evan, Eoin & Bernard Doyle
Macreddin Village, Aughrim
County Wicklow
📱 **+353 (0) 402-36444**
🖑 **www.brooklodge.com**
✉ **brooklodge@macreddin.ie**

The Brook Lodge has been the most dynamically creative hotel in Ireland over the last decade, a blast of brilliant authenticity.

The Brook Lodge is a world unto itself, an idealised world where everything – everything! – is as good as it can possibly be. Evan Doyle and his crew are the most determined, most autodidactic bunch you could ever meet. Whatever they do has to be done the best, and it's not enough that they run the best hotel, where everything you eat is certified organic, and sourced with the most meticulous thoroughness. They also run an authentic Italian restaurant, La Taverna Armento, also of organic standard and dedicated to Italian cooking from Basilicata. They run the most fabulous farmers' market in the grounds, a jamboree of great foods, great fun and great people. The Brook Lodge is a wonderful place to organise a work meeting, and it's a wonderful location in which to get married. Evan Doyle is the most dedicated and capable hotelier of his generation, and his achievement in the Brook Lodge is one of the glories of Irish hospitality, an authentic experience, a truly original experience.

- **OPEN:** All year, including Christmas
- **ROOMS:** 90 rooms and suites
- **PRICE:** €70-€135 per person sharing, single supplement €45. Also web offers.

- **NOTES:** All major cards accepted. Restaurant, pub, market and bakery. Secure car parking. Reservations essential. Limited wheelchair access.

- **DIRECTIONS:**
N11 to Rathnew. Right at r'about, to Glenealy, on to Rathdrum. 1.5km outside Rathdrum, right towards Aughrim. GPS 52.8796666 -6.3315

Northern Ireland

ANNA'S HOUSE

Anna Johnson
Tullynagee, 35 Lisbarnett Rd
Comber, County Down
☎ **+44 (0) 28-9754 1566**
🖰 **www.annashouse.com**
📩 **anna@annashouse.com**

Anna Johnson's house is cult classic, built on the foundations of brilliant cooking with organic ingredients.

Anna Johnson opened her house to guests in the year 2000, so this year marks a decade of superlative hospitality from this superlative cook, hostess and housekeeper. Mrs Johnson's foundation for accommodating guests is simple, and fundamental: ask what influenced her the most, and she says "The family ethos of cooking everything from scratch, and cooking with love". There you have it, in one sentence. And everything you eat in Anna's House is cooked from scratch, cooked with love, and you can taste it: you really can.

Mrs Johnson's B&B is celebrated because it is the B&B of your dreams. A gorgeous, welcoming house. Beautiful gardens. Superlative cooking. And the sort of maternal care for every guest that is beyond price, making Anna's not just a global brand, but a true global luxury brand. After just half an hour here, it is impossible to believe that Belfast is only 14 miles away. After an hour, it's impossible to believe that anywhere else exists at all.

● **OPEN:** All year, except Christmas
● **ROOMS:** Four rooms
● **PRICE:** £85-£95 per room, double occupancy, £55-£65 single occupancy. 5% charge for accepting Visa.

● **NOTES:**
Visa, Mastercard, Switch, Maestro. No dinner. Secure car parking. Wheelchair access. Babies welcome, not suitable for children (lake). Wi-Fi Internet access.

● **DIRECTIONS:**
In Lisbane pass petrol station, turn right into Lisbarnett Rd. After 1km follow concrete lane leading up the hill.

BEECH HILL HOUSE HOTEL

Patsey O'Kane
Londonderry
County Londonderry

📱 **+44 (0) 28-7134 9279**
🖰 **www.beech-hill.com**
✉ **info@beech-hill.com**

Patsey O'Kane is one of the greatest hoteliers, and one of the most important figures in Northern Ireland's unique culture of hospitality.

We are unashamed admirers of Patsey O'Kane. She is one of the great figures of Northern Irish hospitality, incarnating that true hospitality that the Northerners exude, but framing it within the tenets of acute professionalism, and within the lovely aesthetic of Beech Hill House itself. Ms O'Kane is to Northern hospitality what Myrtle Allen is to Southern hospitality: an original, a person of true conviction, a shining, modest star. What makes the Beech Hill special is simple, and utterly fundamental: everyone in the hotel over-delivers, everyone is always trying to do their best, to make sure that every detail is done right, done as well as it can be. That is the art of hotel keeping, that is the very essence of the art we look for in the Bridgestone Guides, and Ms O'Kane is mistress of that art and testifies to that art every day in her work in this beautiful, early 18th-century house. Beech Hill is only two miles from Derry, but truthfully it is a place of and unto itself, a place of hospitality. Dame Patsey O'Kane, everyone? Let it be!

● **OPEN:** All year, except 24-25 Dec
● **ROOMS:** 27 rooms and suites
● **PRICE:** B&B £115-£230 per person sharing, £95-£105 single

● **NOTES:**
All major cards accepted. Ardmore Restaurant open for lunch and dinner. Wheelchair accessible.

● **DIRECTIONS:**
On the A6 direction in Londonderry, take the turning off at Faughan Bridge. Travel 1 mile to Ardmore Chapel, where you will see the hotel entrance on your left.

THE CARRIAGE HOUSE

Maureen Griffith
71 Main Street, Dundrum
County Down
☎ **+44 (0) 28-4375 1635**
🖱 **www.carriagehousedundrum.com**
📪 **inbox@carriagehousedundrum.com**

"Thank you for all the delightful guests you have sent my way", says Maureen Griffith. Delightful guests, in the delightful Carriage House. Fab!

South County Down – drumlin country – is one of those areas of Ireland that will, someday soon, and deservedly, be discovered by folk from the Republic. Golfers know it, of course, but for walkers and nature lovers this area is something of a paradise, unspoilt. The jewel of hospitality to match the jewel nature of the area is Maureen Griffith's Carriage House, in lovely Dundrum. A pioneering restaurateur – Mrs Griffith originally ran the Buck's Head Inn, today masterminded brilliantly by Alison and Michael Carruthers – before creating the ravishing visual palette that is the Carriage House. We use the term palette because everything here is painterly, and painterly perfect. Ms Griffith has the aesthete's eye, and the perfectionist's rigour, so house and garden and cooking are all of a superb standard. Add in the mix of places to eat in the village, and Dundrum offers all you need for a superlative base. Mind you, after breakfast in the Carriage, you may feel like doing not much at all...

● **OPEN:** All year
● **ROOMS:** Three rooms, all en suite
● **PRICE:** £75 double room, including breakfast, Single room £45

● **NOTES:** No credit cards. No dinner, but two excellent restaurants, adjacent to building. Storage for guests' bicycles. No wheelchair access, bedrooms on second floor. Postcode BT330LU

● **DIRECTIONS:**
Dundrum is on the main Belfast to Newcastle road (A24), and The Carriage House is in the centre of town.

DUFFERIN COACHING INN

Leontine Haines
Killyleagh
County Down
📞 **+44 (0) 28-4482 1134**
🖥 www.dufferincoachinginn.com
✉ info@dufferincoachinginn.com

A great new arrival, the
Dufferin Coaching Inn is
handsome, professional,
polished and pretty.

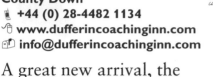

Something new

Leontine Haines has gotten all the details right in this lovely coaching house in pretty Killyleagh, part of which was formerly a bank. Unlike most Irish banks, however, Ms Haines knows how to run a business properly: no short selling here! The rooms and bathrooms are beautifully appointed, the towels are fluffy, the Bircher muesli at breakfast is as scrumptious as all the other homemade ingredients that comprise the feast that starts the day. Most guests will choose to eat next door at the excellent Dufferin Arms, where the cooking is very good indeed, but Ms Haines has already offered some themed dinners for guests, and there are plans to have a more formal dinner offer in the near future. If the dinners are as good as all the other elements of this super-swish operation, it will be another feather in the cap of this lovely village in this lovely region. Wine buffs, by the way, shouldn't miss a visit to Jim Nicholson's stunning wine shop in nearby Crossgar, the most beautiful wine shop in Ireland, another good reason to get down to Killyleagh.

● **OPEN:** All year
● **ROOMS:** Seven rooms, all en-suite
● **PRICE:** B&B £60-£90 per room (£40-£55 for single occupancy)

● **NOTES:** All major cards accepted. No wheelchair access.

● **DIRECTIONS:**
Killyleagh is 16 miles, half an hour's drive, from Belfast, and the Inn is in the town centre, next to the Dufferin Arms.

MARLAGH LODGE

Robert & Rachel Thompson
71 Moorfields Road, Ballymena
County Antrim
📞 **+44 (0) 28-2563 1505**
🖱 **www.marlaghlodge.com**
✉ **info@marlaghlodge.com**

Rachel Thompson's cooking is the star of Marlagh Lodge, and it's some of the very best country cooking.

Renovated from being a virtual ruin just a few years ago, Marlagh Lodge shows both the temperament of Robert and Rachel Thompson – determined, dogged, meticulous, gifted with a true and original aesthetic vision – and shows also their other-worldliness. The time frame of Marlagh doesn't belong in this century, with its daft freneticism. Instead, the time frame here is maybe mid-Edwardian – Henry James; Chesterton; H.G. Wells. There's a happy hen and rooster, with the imposing, not to say confusing, names of Dido and Belinda, strolling around the walled courtyard garden, for example, another delightful distraction in this delightful house. The other prodigious charm of the house is Rachel's stunning cooking, with its gracious flavour notes cascading from every dish. Mrs Thompson's food puts us in mind of Diana Henry's cooking, bullet-pointed with vivid flavour accents from starters through main dishes and on to puddings; the cherry on the icing of a great confection.

● **OPEN:** Open all year, except Christmas
● **ROOMS:** Three rooms, all en suite
● **PRICE:** B&B £50 per person

● **NOTES:**
Mastercard, Visa, Switch, Maestro. Dinner, 8pm £32.50 (book by noon). No wheelchair access.

● **DIRECTIONS:**
From the A36 to Larne, turn onto Rankinstown Road, and the driveway is immediately on your left.
GPS 54.846111 -6.226944

Index

CONTACT THE BRIDGESTONE GUIDES:

We greatly appreciate receiving reports, e-mails and criticisms from readers, and would like to thank those who have written in the past, whose opinions are of enormous assistance to us when considering which 100 places finally make it into this book.

Our website has two contact forms - one to contact us, and the other to make recommendations.

We love hearing from you.

www.bridgestoneguides.com

twitter

facebook

KEEP IN TOUCH WITH THE WORLD OF IRISH FOOD:

Who's Who in Irish Food: read a comprehensive listing

at www.bridgestoneguides.com

Follow Bridgestone Guides on
Facebook - we are Bridgestone Guides
Twitter - we are BridgestoneEd

John McKenna blogs at www.bridgestoneguides.com